W9-ABM-267

Contents

tanti ringraziamenti a Bianca Garufi
e ai miei amici italiani

Foreword

This monograph was written during the Autumn of 1979 at the request of the Istituto dell'Enciclopedia Italiana for inclusion in Volume V (pages 813–27) of the *Enciclopedia del Novecento*, published in 1981, where it can be read in the Italian translation of Bianca Garufi. Her assiduous attention helped these condensed formulations find their final expression.

Though I feel ambivalent about these sorts of abbreviations, it seemed to me that since it was out in translation why not in the original. For this first publication in English, I have made scarcely any revisions, neither bringing the literature up-to-date (other than a few insertions), nor enumerating the directions archetypal psychology has taken in various hands since 1979, nor reporting on lectures, conferences, meetings. Developments move so quickly that the fantasy of 'keeping-up-to-date' is misplaced. Rather, this essay serves merely to locate archetypal psychology as a topic of thought presented in the style of an encyclopedia of the twentieth century.

To supplement this monograph with its own full bibliography, there is appended a complete checklist of my writings, including translations and unpublished papers, which replaces and extends the one concluding in 1975 that was available in *Loose Ends*.

I am extremely grateful to Robert Scott Dupree for his masterful work with the checklist, to Susan Dupree who expertly and caringly composed the text, and to Mary Helen Gray for supervising the editing and production of the entire work. She made this book.

Dallas, October 1982   J. H.

Part One

1   Sources of Archetypal Psychology

Archetypal psychology, first named as such by Hillman (1970b), had from its beginning the intention of moving beyond clinical inquiry within the consulting room of psychotherapy by situating itself within the culture of Western imagination. It is a psychology deliberately affiliated with the arts, culture, and the history of ideas, arising as they do from the imagination. The term "archetypal," in contrast to "analytical" which is the usual appellation for Jung's psychology, was preferred not only because it reflected "the deepened theory of Jung's later work which attempts to solve psychological problems beyond scientific models" (Hillman 1970b); it was preferred more importantly because "archetypal" belongs to all culture, all forms of human activity, and not only to professional practitioners of modern therapeutics. By traditional definition, archetypes are the primary forms that govern the psyche. But they cannot be contained only by the psyche, since they manifest as well in physical, social, linguistic, aesthetic, and spiritual modes. Thus, archetypal psychology's first links are with culture and imagination rather than with medical and empirical psychologies, which tend to confine psychology to the positivistic manifestations of the nineteenth-century condition of the soul.

Archetypal psychology can be seen as a cultural movement part of whose task is the re-visioning of psychology, psychopathology, and psychotherapy in terms of the Western cultural imagination.

In an early review of the field and an examination of its main thrusts, Goldenberg (1975) regards archetypal psychology as a "third generation" derivative of the Jungian school in which Jung is recognized as the source but not as the doctrine. Two themes of its directions which she singles out—the emphasis upon psychopathology and the radical relativization and desubstantiation of the ego—will be discussed below.

It is without doubt that the first immediate father of archetypal psychology is Carl Gustav Jung, the Swiss psychologist (1875–1961). Hillman, Lopez-Pedraza, Berry, Kugler, M. Stein, Guggenbühl, Garufi, Grinnell, and many others of the authors referred to below were trained as Jungian analysts. (However, a significant number of other authors mentioned —e.g., Miller, Casey, Durand, Watkins, Sardello—did not receive this specific Jungian formation and contribute to archetypal psychology from phenomenology, literature, poetry, philosophy, religious studies, etc.) From Jung comes the idea that the basic and universal structures of the psyche, the formal patterns of its relational modes, are archetypal patterns. These are like psychic organs, congenitally given with the psyche itself (yet not necessarily genetically inherited), even if somewhat modified by historical and geographical factors. These patterns or *archai* appear in the arts, religions, dreams, and social customs of all peoples, and they manifest spontaneously in mental disorders. For Jung, they are anthropological and cultural, and also spiritual in that they transcend the empirical world of time and place and, in fact, are in themselves not phenomenal. Archetypal psychology, in distinction to Jungian, considers the archetypal to be always phenomenal (Avens 1980), thus avoiding the Kantian idealism implied in Jung (de Voogd 1977).

The primary, and irreducible, language of these archetypal patterns is the metaphorical discourse of myths. These can therefore be understood as the most fundamental patterns of human existence. To study human nature at its most basic level, one must turn to culture (mythology, religion, art, architecture, epic, drama, ritual) where these patterns are portrayed. The full implication of this move away from bio-chemical, socio-historical, and personal-behavioristic bases for human nature and toward the imaginative has been artic-ulated by Hillman as "the poetic basis of mind" (q.v.). Sup-port for the archetypal and psychological significance of myth, besides the work of Jung, comes from Ernst Cassirer, Karl Kerényi, Erich Neumann, Heinrich Zimmer, Gilbert Durand, Joseph Campbell, and David Miller.

The second immediate father of archetypal psychology is Henry Corbin (1903–1978), the French scholar, philosopher, and mystic, principally known for his interpretation of Islamic thought. From Corbin (1971–73) comes the idea that the *mundus archetypalis* (*'alam al-mithāl*) is also the *mundus im-aginalis*. It is a distinct field of imaginal realities requiring methods and perceptual faculties different from the spiritual world beyond it or the empirical world of usual sense percep-tion and naive formulation. The *mundus imaginalis* offers an ontological mode of locating the archetypes of the psyche, as the fundamental structures of the imagination or as fun-damentally imaginative phenomena that are transcendent to the world of sense in their *value* if not their appearance. Their value lies in their theophanic nature and in their vir-tuality or potentiality which is always ontologically more than actuality and its limits. (As phenomena they must appear, though this appearance is to the imagination or in the imagination.) The *mundus imaginalis* provides for archetypes a valuative and cosmic grounding, when this is needed, different from such bases as: biological instinct, eternal forms, numbers, linguistic and social transmission, biochemical reactions, genetic coding, etc.

But more important than the ontological placing of archetypal realities is the double move of Corbin: (a) that the fundamental nature of the archetype is accessible to imagination first and first presents itself as image, so that (b) the entire procedure of archetypal psychology as a method is imaginative. Its exposition must be rhetorical and poetic, its reasoning not logical, and its therapeutic aim neither social adaptation nor personalistic individualizing but rather a work in service of restoration of the patient to imaginal realities. The aim of therapy (q.v.) is the development of a sense of soul, the middle ground of psychic realities, and the method of therapy is the cultivation of imagination.

In extending the tradition of Jung and Corbin forward, archetypal psychology has had to go back to their predecessors, particularly the Neoplatonic tradition via Vico and the Renaissance (Ficino), through Proclus and Plotinus, to Plato (*Phaedo, Phaedrus, Meno, Symposium, Timaeus*), and most anciently to Heraclitus. (Corbin's works on Avicenna, Ibn' Arabi, and Sohrawardi belong also in this tradition as does the work of Kathleen Raine on William Blake [1758–1835] and on Thomas Taylor, the English translator of the main writings of Plato and the Neoplatonists.)

The elaboration of this tradition by Hillman in Eranos lectures and in articles (1973a), by Miller in seminars at Syracuse University, by Lopez-Pedraza at the University of Caracas, and by Moore's (1982) and Boer's (1980) work on Ficino gives a different cast to archetypal psychology when compared with Jung's. There the background is more strongly German (Nietzsche, Schopenhauer, Carus, von Hartmann, Kant, Goethe, Eckhart, and Böhme), Christian, psychiatric, and Eastern. Archetypal psychology situates itself more comfortably *south* (q.v.) of the Alps.

Especially—this Neoplatonic tradition is thoroughly Western even if it is not empirical in method, rationalist in conception, or otherworldly spiritual in appeal. This tradition holds to the notion of soul as a first principle, placing this soul as a *tertium* between the perspectives of body (matter, nature, empirics) and of mind (spirit, logic, idea). Soul as *tertium*, the perspective *between* others and from which others may be viewed, has been described as Hermetic consciousness (Lopez-Pedraza 1977), as *"esse in anima"* (Jung [1921] CW 6, §66, 77), as the position of the *mundus imaginalis* by Corbin, and by Neoplatonic writers on the intermediaries or figures of the *metaxy*. Body, soul, spirit: this tripartite anthropology further separates archetypal psychology from the usual Western dualistic division, whose history goes back before Descartes to at least the ninth century (869: Eighth General Council at Constantinople), occurring also in the mediaeval ascension of Averroes's Aristotelianism over Avicenna's Platonism. Consequences of this dualistic division are still being felt in that the psyche has become indistinguishable from bodily life, on the one hand, or from the life of the spirit on the other. In the dualistic tradition, psyche never had its own logos. There could be no true psychology. A first methodologically consistent attempt to articulate one in a *philosophical* style belongs also within the perimeters of archetypal psychology (Christou 1963).

2   *Image and Soul: The Poetic Basis of Mind*

The datum with which archetypal psychology begins is the image. The image was identified with the psyche by Jung ("image *is* psyche"—CW 13, §75), a maxim which archetypal psychology has elaborated to mean that the soul is constituted of images, that the soul is primarily an imagining activity most natively and paradigmatically presented by the dream. For it is in the dream that the dreamer himself performs as one image among others and where it can legitimately be shown that the dreamer is in the image rather than the image in the dreamer.

The source of images—dream-images, fantasy-images, poetic-images—is the self-generative activity of the soul itself. In archetypal psychology the word "image," therefore, does not refer to an after-image, the result of sensations and perceptions; nor does "image" mean a mental construct that represents in symbolic form certain ideas and feelings which it expresses. In fact, the image has no referent beyond itself, neither proprioceptive, external, nor semantic: "images don't stand for anything" (Hillman 1978a). They are the psyche itself in its imaginative visibility; as primary datum, image is irreducible. (The relation of image and "structure" has been discussed by Berry 1974 and by Kugler 1979b.)

Visibility, however, need not mean that an image must be visually seen. It does not have to have hallucinatory properties which confuse the act of perceiving images with imagining them. Nor do images have to be heard as in a poetic passage. Such notions of "visibility" tend to literalize images as distinct events presented to the senses. Hence Casey

(1974), in his path-breaking essay "Toward an Archetypal Imagination," states that an image is not what one sees but the way in which one sees. An image is given by the imagining perspective and can only be perceived by an act of imagining.

The autochthonous quality of images as *independent* (Watkins 1981, pp. 124f.) of the subjective imagination which does the perceiving takes Casey's idea one step further. *First,* one believes images are hallucinations (things seen); *then* one recognizes them as acts of subjective imagining; but then, *third,* comes the awareness that images are independent of subjectivity and even of the imagination itself as a mental activity. Images come and go (as in dreams) at their own will, with their own rhythm, within their own fields of relations, undetermined by personal psychodynamics. In fact, images are the fundamentals which make the movements of psychodynamics possible. They claim reality, that is, authority, objectivity, and certainty. In this third recognition, the mind is in the imagination rather than the imagination in the mind. The noetic and the imaginal no longer oppose each other (Hillman 1981a, b). "Yet this is still 'psychology' although no longer science; it is psychology in the wider meaning of the word, a psychological activity of creative nature, in which creative fantasy is given prior place" (Jung, CW 6, §84).

Corbin (1958) attributes this recognition to the awakened heart as locus of imagining, a locus also familiar in the Western tradition from Michelangelo's *immagine del cuor.* This interdependence of heart and image intimately ties the very basis of archetypal psychology with the phenomena of love (q.v. eros). Corbin's theory of creative imagination of the heart further implies for psychology that, when it bases itself in the image, it must at the same time recognize that imagination is not merely a human faculty but is an activity of soul to which the human imagination bears witness. It is not we who imagine but we who are imagined.

When "image" is thus transposed from a human representation of its conditions to a sui generis activity of soul in independent presentation of its bare nature, all empirical studies on imagination, dream, fantasy, and the creative process in artists, as well as methods of *rêve dirigé*, will contribute little to a psychology of the image if they start with the empirics of imagining rather than with the phenomenon of the image—which is not a product of imagining. Empirical approaches of analyzing and guiding images strive to gain control over them. Archetypal psychology distinguishes itself radically from these methods of image control as has been cogently argued by Watkins (1976, 1981). Casey's turning of the notion of image from something seen to a way of seeing (a seeing of the heart—Corbin) offers archetypal psychology's solution to an old dilemma between true *(vera)* imagination (Paracelsus) and false, or fancy (Coleridge). For archetypal psychology, the distinction depends upon the way in which the image is responded to and worked. The criteria it uses, therefore, refer to *response*: metaphorical and imaginative as being a better response than fanciful or literal and this because, where the former response is "fecund" (Langer), furthering the deepening and elaboration of the image, the latter responses dissipate or program the image into more naive, shallow, or fixedly dogmatic significance.

For archetypal psychology, images are neither good nor bad, true nor false, demonic nor angelic (Hillman 1977a), though an image always implicates "a precisely qualified context, mood and scene" (as Hillman [1977b] has on one occasion defined the image). Thus they do invite judgment as a further precision of the image, judgment arising from the image itself as an effect of the image's own presentation of a claim for response. To suspend judgment, therefore, is to fall into the objectivist fantasy. Judgments are inherent to the image (as a work of art brings with it the standards by which it can be measured or a text brings with it the hermeneutics by which it can be interpreted). Archetypal psychology examines the judgments about the image imagistically, regarding them as its further specifications and as psychological statements not to be taken literally from a spiritual (q.v.), purely noetic, vantage point detached from the context of the image judged.

The emphasis upon response has led archetypal psychology to use the analogy of the craftsman when discussing moral judgments. How well has the image worked; does the image release and refine further imagining? Does the response "stick to the image" (Lopez-Pedraza) as the task at hand, rather than associate or amplify into non-imagistic symbolisms, personal opinions, and interpretations? Such are the questions asked by archetypal psychology.

"Stick to the image" (cf. Jung, *CW* 16, §320) has become a golden rule of archetypal psychology's method, and this because the image is the primary psychological datum. Though the image always implies more than it presents, "the depth of the image—its limitless ambiguities . . . can only be partly grasped as implications. So to expand upon the dream image is also to narrow it—a further reason we wish never to stray too far from the source" (Berry 1974, p. 98).

It must be noted that the "source" is *complex*: archetypal psychology is complex at the beginning, since the image is a self-limiting multiple relationship of meanings, moods, historical events, qualitative details, and expressive possibilities. As its referent is imaginal, it always retains a virtuality beyond its actuality (Corbin 1977, p. 167). An image always seems more profound (archetypal), more powerful (potential), and more beautiful (theophanic) than the com- prehension of it, hence the feeling, while recording a dream, of seeing through a glass darkly. Hence, too, the driving necessity in the arts, for they provide complicated disciplines that can actualize the complex virtuality of the image.

This polysemous complexity bespeaks a polytheistic (q.v.) psychology of personifications analogous with Jung's theory of complexes as the multiple consciousness at the base of psychic life (CW 8, §388ff.). By starting with a complex datum, the image, archetypal psychology is saved from accounting for psychic life in simplistic terms of elementary mechanisms, primordialities of origins, or numerically limited basic struc- tures. Reductionism is defeated from the start because the mind is poetic to begin with, and consciousness is not a later, secondary elaboration upon a primitive base but is given with that base in each image.

The "poetic basis of mind" was a thesis Hillman (1975a, p. xi) first set forth in his 1972 Terry Lectures at Yale Univer- sity and which states that archetypal psychology "starts neither in the physiology of the brain, the structure of language, the organization of society, nor the analysis of behavior, but in processes of imagination." The inherent relation between psychology and the cultural imagination is necessitated by the nature of mind. The most fecund ap- proach to the study of mind is thus through its highest imagi- national responses (Hough 1973; Giegerich 1982; Berry 1982) where the images are most fully released and elaborated.

3   *Archetypal Image*

Archetypal psychology *axiomatically* assumes imagistic universals, comparable to the *universali fantastici* of Vico (*S.N.* II, I, 1:381), that is, mythical figures that provide the poetic characteristics of human thought, feeling, and action, as well as the physiognomic intelligibility of the qualitative worlds of natural phenomena. By means of the archetypal image, natural phenomena present faces that speak to the imagining soul rather than only conceal hidden laws and probabilities and manifest their objectification.

A psychological universal must be considered *psychologically*. An archetypal image is psychologically 'universal' because its effect amplifies and de-personalizes. Even if the notion of image (q.v.) regards each image as an individualized, unique event, as "that image there and no other," such an image is universal because it resonates with collective, trans-empirical importance. Thus, archetypal psychology uses 'universal' as an adjective, declaring a substantive perduring *value* which ontology states as a hypostasis. And, the universals problem for psychology is not whether they exist, where, and how they participate in particulars, but rather whether a personal individual event can be recognized as bearing essential and collective importance. Psychologically, the universals problem is presented by the soul itself whose perspective is harmoniously both the narrow particularity of felt experience and the universality of archetypally human experience. In Neoplatonic thought, soul could be spoken of as both my soul and world soul, and what was true of one was true of both. Thus, the universality of an archetypal image means also that the response to the image implies more than personal consequences, raising the soul itself beyond its egocentric confines (q.v. soul-making) and broadening the events of nature from discrete atomic particulars to aesthetic signatures bearing information for soul.

Because archetypal psychology gives priority to particular pattern over literal particle—and considers that particular events are always themselves imagistic and therefore ensouled—imagination too is assumed to be primordially patterned into typical themes, motifs, regions, genres, syndromes. These kinds of patterns inform all psychic life. Gilbert Durand (1960, 1979)—following upon the lines opened by Bachelard—and Durand's *centre de recherche sur l'imaginaire* at Chambery have been charting the inherent organization of the imaginary as the basis of cultural anthropology and sociology, even as the basis of psychological meaning in all consciousness. Durand's papers published in the *Eranos Yearbooks* since 1964 present a range of archetypal cultural analysis.

Archetypal psychology has pressed beyond the collection of objective data and the correlation of images as verbal or visual symbols. If archetypal images are the fundamentals of fantasy, they are the means by which the world is imagined, and therefore they are the modes by which all knowledge, all experiences whatsoever become possible. "Every psychic process is an image and an 'imagining', otherwise no consciousness could exist. . . " (*CW* 11, §889). An archetypal image operates like the original meaning of idea (from Greek *eidos* and *eidolon*): not only 'that which' one sees but also that 'by means of which' one sees. The demonstration of archetypal images is therefore as much in the act of seeing as in the object seen, since the archetypal image appears in consciousness itself as the governing fantasy by means of which consciousness is possible to begin with. Gathering of data does less to demonstrate objectively the existence of archetypes than it does to demonstrate the fantasy of "objective data."

Furthermore, unlike Jung, who radically distinguishes between noumenal archetype per se and phenomenal archetypal image, archetypal psychology rigorously refuses even to speculate about a non-presented archetype per se. Its concern is with the phenomenon: the archetypal image. This leads to the next step: ". . . any image can be considered archetypal. The word 'archetypal' . . . rather than pointing *at* something archetypal points *to* something, and this is *value*. . . . by archetypal psychology we mean a psychology of value. And our appellative move is aimed to restore psychology to its widest, richest and deepest volume so that it would resonate with soul [q.v.] in its descriptions as unfathomable, multiple, prior, generative, and necessary. As all images can gain this archetypal sense, so all psychology can be archetypal. . . .'Archetypal' here refers to a move one makes rather than to a thing that is" (Hillman 1977b, pp. 82–83).

Here, archetypal psychology 'sees through' itself as strictly a psychology of archetypes, a mere analysis of structures of being (Gods in their myths), and, by emphasizing the valuative function of the adjective 'archetypal,' restores to images their primordial place as that which gives psychic value to the world. Any image termed 'archetypal' is immediately valued as universal, trans-historical, basically profound, generative, highly intentional, and necessary.

Since 'archetypal' connotes both intentional force (Jung's "instinct") and the mythical field of personifications (Hillman's "Gods"), an archetypal image is animated like an animal (one of Hillman's frequent metaphors for images) and like a person whom one loves, fears, delights in, is inhibited by, and so forth. As intentional force and person, such an

image presents a claim—moral, erotic, intellectual, aesthetic—and demands a response. It is an "affecting presence"
(Armstrong 1971) offering an affective relationship. It seems
to bear prior knowledge (coded information) and an instinc-
tive direction for a destiny, as if prophetic, prognostic. Images in "dreams mean well for us, back us up and urge us on,
understand us more deeply than we understand ourselves,
expand our sensuousness and spirit, continually make up
new things to give us—and this feeling of being loved by the
images . . . call it imaginal love" (Hillman 1979a, p. 196).
This message-bearing experience of the image—and the feeling of blessing that an image can bring—recalls the Neoplatonic sense of images as daimones and angels (message-
bearers). "Perhaps—who knows?—these eternal images are
what men mean by fate" (CW 7, §183).

Although an archetypal image presents itself as impacted
with meaning, this is not given simply as revelation. It must
be *made* through "image work" and "dream work" (Hillman
1977b, 1979a). The modes of this work may be concrete and
physical as in art, movement, play, and occupational thera-
pies; but more importantly (because less fixedly symbolic),
this work is done by "sticking to the image" as a psychological penetration of what is actually presented *including* the
stance of consciousness that is attempting the hermeneutic.
Image work is not legitimately such unless the implicit in-
volvement of a subjective perspective is admitted from the
start, for it too is part of the image and in its fantasy.

Image work requires both aesthetic culture and a background in myths and symbols for appreciation of the univer-
salities of images. This work also requires a series of tactical
moves (Hillman and Berry 1977), frequently linguistic and
phonetic (Sardello et al. 1978; Severson 1978; Kugler 1979b)
and etymological (Lockhart 1978, 1980; Kugelmann), and

also grammatical and syntactical experimentation (Ritsema 1976; Hillman 1978a). Other tactical moves concerning emotion, texture, repetitions, reversals, and restatements have been described by Berry (1974).

The primary intention of this verbal work with images is the "recovery of soul in speech" (Sardello 1978a) which at the same time reveals the erotic and aesthetic aspect of images—that they captivate, charm, persuade, have a rhetorical effect on soul beyond their symbolic content. Image-work restores the original poetic sense to images, freeing them from serving a narrational context, having to tell a story with its linear, sequential, and causal implications that foster first-person reports of the egocentric actions and intentions of a personalistic subject. The distinction between image and narrative (Berry 1974; Miller 1976a) is fundamental to the distinction in imaginative style between archetypal polytheistic (q.v.) psychology and traditional psychologies that are ego-centered, epic narrations (q.v. therapy).

Three further developments in theory of archetypal images are worth attention. Paul Kugler's work (1978, 1979a) elaborates an acoustic theory of images as structures of invariant meaning apart from linguistic, etymological, semantic, and syntactical meaning. Boer and Peter Kugler (1977) have correlated archetypal images with the theory of perception of J. J. Gibson, asserting that archetypal images are afforded directly by the environment (and are not subjective), so that "archetypal psychology is mythical realism." Casey (1979) sets forth the idea that imagination is so closely related with time, both psychologically and ontologically, that actual image-work not only takes time into soul or makes temporal events soul events but also makes time in soul.

4   *Soul*

The primary metaphor of psychology must be soul. Psychology (*logos* of *psyche*) etymologically means: reason or speech or intelligible account of soul. It is psychology's job to find logos for psyche, to provide soul with an adequate account of itself. Psyche as the *anima mundi*, the Neoplatonic soul of the world, is already there with the world itself, so that a second task of psychology is to hear psyche speaking through all things of the world, thereby recovering the world as a place of soul (q.v. soul-making).

In its own speaking about the soul, archetypal psychology maintains an elusive obliqueness (Romanyshyn 1978–79). This continual carefulness not to substantiate soul follows this maxim: "By soul I mean, first of all, a perspective rather than a substance, a viewpoint toward things rather than a thing itself" (Hillman 1975a, p. x). In a long examination of "soul," Hillman (1964) concludes: "The soul is a deliberately ambiguous concept resisting all definition in the same manner as do all ultimate symbols which provide the root metaphors for the systems of human thought." In this same passage, a circumscription of the term states: "We are not able to use the word in an unambiguous way, even though we take it to refer to that unknown human factor which makes meaning possible, which turns events into experiences, and which is communicated in love." In 1967a, a fourth aspect was added: the soul has a religious concern. And in 1975a (p. x), three further qualifications were adjoined: "First, 'soul' refers to the *deepening* of events into experiences; second, the significance soul makes possible, whether in love or religious concern, derives from its special *relation with death*. And third, by 'soul' I mean the imaginative possibility in our natures, the experiencing through reflective speculation, dream, image, and *fantasy*—that mode which recognizes all realities as primarily symbolic or metaphorical."

The literalizing and ontologizing dangers attendant upon the elevation of soul to first principle are met by a certain subversive tone in archetypal psychology that speaks of soul events in imagistic, ironic, and even humorous ways (Hillman and Berry 1977). Common to many writers, though different in each—Guggenbühl-Craig, Miller, Ziegler, Lopez-Pedraza, Giegerich, Sardello—is this dark and mordant style. Psyche is kept close to its shadows. There is a continual attempt to break the vessels even as they are being formed.

The term "soul" is also used freely without defining specific usages and senses in order to keep present its full connotative power. And it is used interchangeably with the Greek *psyché*, the Greek mythic figure, Psyche (Apuleius's tale of *Amor and Psyche*), the Germanic *Seele*, and the Latin *anima*. Here, 'anima' in the more specific Jungian description as a personified figure and function of the imagination (E. Jung 1957; Hillman 1973c, 1974b) bestows rich imagery, pathologies, and feeling qualities to what otherwise might become only a philosophical concept.

The human being is set within the field of soul; soul is the metaphor that includes the human. "*Dasein* as *esse in anima* infinitely surpasses man" (Avens 1982a, p. 185). Even if human life is only one manifestation of the psyche, a human life is always a psychological life—which is how archetypal psychology reads the Aristotelian notion of soul as life and the Christian doctrine of the soul as immortal, i.e., beyond the confines of individual limitation. A humanistic or personalistic psychology will always fail the full perspective of soul that extends beyond human, personal behavior. This move which places man within psyche (rather than psyche within man) revisions all human activity whatsoever as psychological. Every piece of human behavior, whatever its manifest and literal content, is always also a psychological statement.

If every statement has psychological content, then every statement may be scrutinized for its psychological significance, for what it means to soul. Speech about soul itself—what it is, its body relations, its origins and development, what it consists in, how it functions—are psychology's concern only because these are the enduring ways the soul gives accounts of itself in conceptual form. They belong to its 'soul-making' (q.v.), its ongoing fantasy activity, and these accounts called 'psychology' ought to be taken fictionally rather than only as positivistic answers about the nature of the soul. The soul can be an object of study only when it is also recognized as the subject studying itself by means of the fictions and metaphors of objectivity. This scrutiny of statements for their psychic implications is a strategical principle of archetypal psychology, providing its tactical method called "psychologizing, or seeing through" (Hillman 1975a, pp. 113–64). The method puts into practice the notion of the unconscious: whatever is stated contains an unconsciousness within the statement. 'Unconscious' takes on the meaning of *implication* and *supposition* (Berry 1974), that is, what is folded in or held beneath. Statements from any field whatsoever thus become psychological, or revelations of psyche, when their literalism is subverted to allow their suppositions to appear. The strategy implies that psychology cannot be limited to being one field among others since psyche itself permeates all fields and things of the world.

Anima and Rhetoric

By speaking of soul as a primary *metaphor*, rather than defining soul substantively and attempting to derive its ontological status from empirical demonstration or theological (metaphysical) argument, archetypal psychology recognizes that psychic reality is inextricably involved with *rhetoric*. The perspective of soul is inseparable from the manner of speaking of soul, a manner which evokes soul, brings it to life, and persuades us into a psychological perspective. In its concern with rhetoric, archetypal psychology has relied on literary and poetic devices to expound its vision, all the while working at "seeing through" the mechanistic and personalistic metaphors employed by other psychology so as to recover soul from those literalisms. The polemical foray into others' preserves is necessary to the rhetorical mode.

Soul and Myth

The primary rhetoric of archetypal psychology is myth. Here, the path had already been pioneered by Freud, Jung, and Cassirer (Avens 1980), and, of course, by a tradition of mythical thinking going back through the Romantics and Vico to Plato. This move toward mythical accounts as a psychological language locates psychology in the cultural imagination. Secondly, these myths are themselves metaphors (or, as Vico said "metaphor . . . is a myth [*fabula*] in brief" [*S.N.* II, II, 2]), so that by relying on myths as its primary rhetoric, archetypal psychology grounds itself in a fantasy that cannot be taken historically, physically, literally. Even if the recollection of mythology is perhaps the single most characteristic move shared by all "archetypalists," the myths themselves are understood as metaphors—never as transcendental metaphysics whose categories are divine figures. As Hillman (1979a) says: "Myths do not ground, they open." The role of myth in archetypal psychology is not to provide an exhaustive catalogue of possible behaviors or to circumscribe the forms of transpersonal energies (in the Neoplatonic sense), but rather to open the questions of life to transpersonal and culturally imaginative reflection. We may thereby see our ordinary lives embedded in and ennobled by the dramatic and world-creative life of mythical figures (Bedford 1981). The study of mythology allows events to be recognized against their mythical background. More important, however, is that the study of mythology enables one to perceive and experience the life of the soul mythically.

5   Soul, Metaphor and Fantasy

The philosophical problem "how to define soul" or how to state a "logos of soul" (Christou 1963) must be viewed in the first place as a psychological phenomenon, one that arises from the soul's own desire for self-knowledge which can best be satisfied in terms of its own constitution: images. Thus the logos of soul, i.e., a true speaking of it, will be in an imagistic style, an account or "*recit*" (Corbin 1979, pp. 43f.) that is through and through metaphorical.

The statement above that "the primary metaphor of psychology must be soul" attempts two things: (a) to state the soul's nature in its own language (metaphor) and (b) to recognize that all statements in psychology about soul are met-aphors. In this way, soul-as-metaphor leads beyond the prob-lem of "how to define soul" and encourages an account of the soul toward imagining itself rather than defining itself. Here, metaphor serves a psychological function: it becomes an in-strument of soul-making (q.v.) rather than a mere "figure of speech," because it transposes the soul's questioning about its nature to a mythopoesis of actual imagining, an ongoing psychological creation (Berry 1982).

Soul-as-metaphor also describes how the soul acts. It per-forms as does a metaphor, transposing meaning and releasing interior, buried significance. Whatever is heard with the ear of soul reverberates with under- and overtones (Moore 1978). The perspective darkens with a deeper light. But this meta-phorical perspective also kills: it brings about the death of naive realism, naturalism, and literal understanding. The relation of soul to death—a theme running all through arche-typal psychology—is thus a function of the psyche's meta-phorical activity. The metaphorical mode does not speak in declarative statements or explain in clear contrasts. It delivers all things to their shadows. So, its perspective defeats any heroic attempt to gain a firm grip on phenomena; in-stead, the metaphorical mode of soul is "elusive, allusive, illu-sive" (Romanyshyn 1977), undermining the very definition of consciousness as intentionality and its history as development.

Human awareness fails in its comprehension not because of original sin or personal neurosis or because of the obstinacy of the objective world to which it is supposedly opposed. Human awareness fails, according to a psychology based on soul, because the soul's metaphorical nature has a suicidal necessity (Hillman 1964), an underworld affiliation (Hillman 1979a), a "morbism" (Ziegler 1980), a destiny—different from dayworld claims—which makes the psyche fundamentally unable to submit to the *hubris* of an egocentric notion of subjectivity as achievement *(Leistung)*, defined as cognition, conation, intention, perception, and so forth.

Thus, that sense of weakness (Lopez-Pedraza 1977, 1982), inferiority (Hillman 1977c), mortification (Berry 1973), masochism (Cowan 1979), darkness (Winquist 1981), and failure (Hillman 1972b) is inherent to the *mode* of metaphor itself which defeats conscious understanding as a control over phenomena. Metaphor, as the soul's *mode* of logos, ultimately results in that abandonment to the given which approximates mysticism (Avens 1980).

The metaphorical transposition—this 'death-dealing' move that at the same time re-awakens consciousness to a sense of soul—is at the heart of archetypal psychology's mission, its world intention. As Freud and Jung both attempted to discover the fundamental 'mistake' in Western culture so as to resolve the misery of man trapped in the decline of the West, so archetypal psychology specifies this mistake as loss of soul which it further identifies with loss of images and the imaginal sense. The result has been an intensification of subjectivity (Durand 1975), showing both in the self-enclosed egocentricity and the hyperactivism, or life-fanaticism, of Western (rather, Northern q.v.) consciousness which has lost its relation with death and the underworld.

That re-imagining and re-animating of the cultural psyche to which archetypal psychology aspires necessitates pathologizing (q.v.), for only this weakening or "falling apart" (Hillman 1975a) breaks through self-enclosed subjectivity and restores it to its depth in soul, allowing soul to reappear again in the world of things.

The re-animation of things by means of metaphor was already indicated by Vico (S.N. II, I, 2) who wrote that "metaphor . . . gives sense and passion to insensate things." As the metaphorical perspective gives new animation to soul, so too it re-vitalizes areas that had been assumed not en-souled and not psychological: the events of the body and medicine, the ecological world, the man-made phenomena of architecture and transportation, education, food, bureau-cratic language and systems. These have all been examined as metaphorical images and have become subject to intense psychological revision by Sardello and his students first at the University of Dallas and subsequently at The Dallas Institute of Humanities and Culture. The metaphorical perspective which revisions worldly phenomena as images can find "sense and passion" where the Cartesian mind sees the mere extension of de-souled insensate objects. In this way, the poetic basis of mind (q.v.) takes psychology out of the confines of laboratory and consulting room, and even beyond the personal subjectivity of the human person, into a psychology of things as objectifications of images with interiority, things as the display of fantasy.

For archetypal psychology, "fantasy" and "reality" change places and values. First, they are no longer opposed. Second, fantasy is never merely mentally subjective but is always being enacted and embodied (Hillman 1972a, pp. xxxix–xl). Third, whatever is physically or literally 'real' is always also a fantasy image. Thus the world of so-called hard factual reality is always also the display of a specifically shaped fantasy, as if to say, along with Wallace Stevens, the American philosopher-poet of imagination on whom archetypal psychology often draws, there is always "a poem at the heart of things." Jung stated the same idea (*CW* 6, §78): "The psyche creates reality everyday. The only expression I can say for this activity is *fantasy*." And he takes the word "fantasy" "from poetic usage" (*CW* 6, §743).

The latest explorations of archetypal psychology—some published in *Spring 1979-82*—have been in the direction of poetics, aesthetics, and literary criticism. This is less the influence of contemporary psychoanalytic concerns with language than it is the re-appraisal of psychology itself as an activity of *poesis* and the fact that fantasy is the archetypal activity of the psyche.

6   *Soul and Spirit*

If imagining is the native activity of the *anima mundi*, then fantasy is always going on and is not subject to a phenomenological *epoché* (Husserl: setting aside or bracketing out in order to move directly to the event itself). Moreover, if fantasy is always going on, then *epoché* is itself a fantasy: of isolating, of objectification, and of a consciousness that can be truly addressed by phenomena as they are. Archetypal psychology maintains, however, that we can never be purely phenomenal or truly objective. One is never beyond the subjectivism given with the soul's native dominants of fantasy structures. These dominate subjective perspectives and organize them into 'stances,' so that the only objectivity that could be approximated results from the subjective eye turned in on itself, regarding its own regard, examining its own perspective for the archetypal subjects (q.v. personifying) who are at this moment governing our way of being in the world among phenomena. Psychology as an objective science is forever impossible once one has recognized that objectivity is itself a poetic genre (similar to "writer-as-mirror" in French naturalism), a mode that constructs the world so that things appear as sheer things (not faces, not animated, not with interiority), subject to will, separate from each other, mute, without sense or passion.

One position is particularly obdurate in yielding to the fantasy that fantasy is always going on, and that is the stance of spirit. It appears as scientific objectivity, as metaphysics, and as theology. And where archetypal psychology has attacked these approaches, it is part of a wider strategy to distinguish the methods and rhetoric of soul from those of spirit, so that soul is not forced to forfeit its style to fulfill the obligations required by a spiritual perspective, whether philosophical, scientific, or religious. For psychology to be possible at all it must keep the distinction between soul and spirit (Hillman 1976; 1975a, pp. 67–70; 1977a).

At times the spirit position with its rhetoric of order, number, knowledge, permanency, and self-defensive logic has been discussed as "senex" and Saturnian (Vitale 1973; Hillman 1975d); at other times, because of its rhetoric of clarity and detached observation, it has been discussed as Apollonic (Hillman 1972c); on other occasions, because of the rhetoric of unity, ultimacy, identity, it has been termed "monotheistic"; and in yet other contexts, "heroic" and also "puer" (1967b).

While recognizing that the spirit perspective must place itself above (as the soul places itself as inferior) and speak in transcendent, ultimate, and pure terms, archetypal psychology conceives its task to be one of imagining the spirit language of "truth," "faith," "law," and the like as a rhetoric of spirit, even if spirit is obliged by this same rhetoric to take its stance truthfully and faithfully, i.e., literally.

The distinction between soul and spirit further guards against psychological therapy becoming confused with spiritual disciplines—whether Eastern or Western—and gives yet another reason for archetypal psychology to eschew borrowings from meditative techniques and/or operant conditioning, both of which conceptualize psychic events in spiritual terms.

7   *Soul-Making*

The underlying aspiration of its work archetypal psychology has called "soul-making," taking the phrase from the poets William Blake and, particularly, John Keats: "Call the world if you please, 'The vale of Soul-making.' Then you will find out the use of the world. . . . " For all its emphasis upon the individualized soul, archetypal psychology sets this soul, and its making, squarely in the midst of the world. And, it does not seek a way out of or beyond the world toward redemption or mystical transcendence, because "The way through the world is more difficult to find than the way beyond it" (Wallace Stevens, "Reply to Papini"). The curative or salvational vision of archetypal psychology focuses upon the soul in the world which is also the soul of the world (*anima mundi*). The idea of soul-making by taking any world event as also a place of soul insists that even this Neoplatonic and 'arcane' psychology is nonetheless embedded in the "vale" and its engagement therein. The artificial tension between soul and world, private and public, interior and exterior thus disappears when the soul as *anima mundi*, and its making, is located in the world.

More specifically, the act of soul-making is imagining, since images are the psyche, its stuff, and its perspective. Crafting

images—such as discussed below in regard to therapy (q.v.)—
is thus an equivalent of soul-making. This crafting can take
place in the concrete modes of the artisan, a work of the
hands, and with the morality of the hands. And, it can take
place in sophisticated elaborations of reflection, religion, relationships, social action, so long as these activities are imagined from the perspective of soul, soul as uppermost concern.

In other words, only when imagination is recognized as an
engagement at the borders of the human and a work in relation with mythic dominants can this articulation of images
be considered a psycho-poesis (Miller 1976b) or soul-making.
Its intention is the realization of the images—for they are the
psyche—and not merely of the human subject. As Corbin
has said: "It is their individuation, not ours," suggesting that
soul-making can be most succinctly defined as the individuation of imaginal reality.

Soul-making is also described as imaging, that is, seeing or
hearing by means of an imagining which sees through an
event to its image. Imaging means releasing events from their
literal understanding into a mythical appreciation. Soul-
making, in this sense, is equated with de-literalizing—that
psychological attitude which suspiciously disallows the naive
and given level of events in order to search out their
shadowy, metaphorical significances for soul.

So the question of soul-making is "what does this event,
this thing, this moment move in my soul? What does it mean
to my death?" The question of death enters because it is in
regard to death that the perspective of soul is distinguished
most starkly from the perspective of natural life.

Soul-making does imply a metaphysical fantasy, and the
implied metaphysics of archetypal psychology are best found
in *The Dream and the Underworld* (Hillman 1979a) which
elaborates the relations between psyche and death. There the

dream is taken as the paradigm of the psyche—where the psyche presents itself encompassing the ego and engaged in its own work (dream-work). From the dream, one may assume that the psyche is fundamentally concerned with its imaginings and only secondarily concerned with subjective experiences in the dayworld which the dream transforms into images, i.e., into soul. The dream is thus making soul each night. Images become the means of translating life-events into soul, and this work, aided by the conscious elaboration of imagination, builds an imaginal vessel, or "ship of death" (a phrase taken from D. H. Lawrence), that is similar to the subtle body, or *ochema* of the Neoplatonists (cf. Avens 1982b). The question of the soul's immortality is not directly answered by a metaphysical statement. Rather, the very nature of the soul in the dream—or at least the perspective of soul toward the dream—shows its inattention to and disregard for mortal experience as such, even for physical death itself, receiving into its purview only those faces and events from the mortal world that bear upon the opus of its destiny.

8   *Depth and the Vertical Direction*

Since its beginning in Freud's study of the deep layers of the mind—pre-, sub-, or un-conscious—the field of "depth psychology" (so named at the turn of the century by the Zürich psychiatrist Eugen Bleuler) has always been directed downward, whether toward buried memories of childhood or toward archaic mythologems. Archetypal psychology has taken this depth metaphor equally seriously—though less literally. It has carried the metaphor of depth of soul back in history to Heraclitus (Diels–Kranz, Frag. 45: *bathun*) and then to Augustine's *thesaurus* or *memoria* (*Confessions* X). Moreover, it has reverted Freud's own move into depth, the descent into the dream as described in his *Traumdeutung*, to the mythologies of the Underworld, Hades, Persephone, Dionysus—and to Christian theologies of descent (Miller 1981b)—exploring the fundamental relation of the psyche with the realm of the dead which is also the realm of images or *eidola* (Hillman 1979a).

Because of the vertical direction of depth psychology, it is obliged to be concerned with depression and with the reduction of phenomena to their 'deadly' essence, their pathologized (q.v.) extremity (Berry 1973), where we experience them as both materially destructive and negative and yet as the ground of support (Berry 1978b).

The literalization of downwardness in depth psychology has resulted in a narrowness of meaning: introverted inwardness within the person, into the "abyss" and "secret chamber" of the personal self (Augustine). What then of the relationship with others, with the horizontal world?

For archetypal psychology, the vertical direction refers to interiority as a capacity within all things. All things have an archetypal significance and are available to psychological penetration, and this interiority is manifested by the physiognomic character of the things of the horizontal world. Depth is therefore not literally hidden, deep down, inside. Rather, the fantasy of depth encourages us to look at the world again, to read each event for 'something deeper,' to "insearch" (Hillman 1967a), rather than to research, for yet further significance below what seems merely evident and natural. The downward interiorizing fantasy is thus at the very basis of all psychoanalysis. The fantasy of hidden depths ensouls the world and fosters imagining ever deeper into things. Depth—rather than a literal or physical location—is a primary metaphor necessary for psychological thinking (or "psychologizing," Hillman 1975a).

9   *Cultural Locus: North and South*

The downward direction may also be envisioned as Southward. Unlike the main psychologies of the twentieth century which have drawn their sources from Northern Europe—the German language and the Protestant-Jewish monotheistic Weltanschauung—archetypal psychology starts in the South. Neither Greek nor Renaissance civilization developed "psychologies" as such. The word "psychology" and most modern psychological terms (Hillman 1972c) do not appear in an active sense until the nineteenth century. In recognition of these historical facts, archetypal psychology situates its work in a pre-psychological geography, where the culture of imagination and the modes of living carried what had to be formulated in the North as "psychology." "Psychology" is a necessity of a post-reformational culture that had been deprived of its poetic base.

Since, as Casey (1982) maintains, place is prior to the possibility of thought—all thought must be placed in order to be—archetypal psychology requires an imaginal location. Freud's 'Vienna' and Jung's 'Zürich,' or the 'California Schools' are fantasy locations, not merely sociological and historical contexts. They place the ideas in a geographical image. Such is "south" in the imagination of archetypal psychology.

"South" is both an ethnic, cultural, geographic place and a symbolic one. It is both the Mediterranean culture, its images and textual sources, its sensual and concrete humanity, its Gods and Goddesses and their myths, its tragic and picaresque genres (rather than the epic heroism of the North); and it is a symbolic stance "below the border" which does not view that region of the soul only from a northern moralistic perspective. The unconscious thus becomes radically re-visioned and may as well be located 'up north' (as Aryan, Apollonic, Germanic, positivistic, voluntaristic, rationalistic, Cartesian, protestant, scientistic, personalistic, monotheistic, etc.). Even the family, rather than a source of 'northern' neurosis, can be revalued as the ground of ancestral and societal binding.

By remembering this fundamental division in Western cultural history, archetypal psychology eludes the conventional dilemma of "East and West." Positions usually given over to the "East" are included within archetypal psychology's own orientation. Having re-oriented consciousness toward non-ego factors—the multiple personifications of the soul, the elaboration of the imaginal ground of myths, the direct immediacy of sense experience coupled with the ambiguity of its interpretation, and the radically relative phenomenality of the 'ego' itself as but one fantasy of the psyche—archetypal psychology makes superfluous the move toward oriental disciplines which have had to be found in the East when psychology is identified with the perspectives of northern psychic geography.

Roberts Avens's monographs (1980, 1982a, b) show that archetypal psychology is nothing less than a parallel formulation of certain Eastern philosophies. Like them, it too dissolves ego, ontology, substantiality, literalisms of self and divisions between it and things—the entire conceptual apparatus which northern psychology constructs from the heroic ego and in its defense—into the psychic reality of imagination experienced in immediacy. The 'emptying out' of Western positivisms, comparable to a Zen exercise or a way of Nirvana, is precisely what archetypal psychology has effectuated, though by means that are utterly Western, where 'Western' refers to a psychology of soul as imagined in the tradition of the South.

10   *Polytheistic Psychology and Religion*

Of all the moves, none is so far-reaching in cultural implication as the attempt to recover the perspectives of polytheism. Moore (1980) considers this perspective to be the rational consequent of a psychology based in *anima* which can "animate" the study of religion by offering both "a way of understanding religion . . . and a way of going about religious studies" (p. 284). Miller's christology (1981a) demonstrates the relevance of the polytheistic perspective for even a religion whose dogma historically derives from an anti-polytheistic position. The complex issues of the new polytheism have been treated by Miller (1974, with an appendix by Hillman 1981) and by Goldenberg (1979). The polytheistic moves of archetypal psychology occur in four interrelated modes.

(1) The most accurate model of human existence will be able to account for its innate diversity, both among individuals and within each individual. Yet, this same model must also provide fundamental structures and values for this

diversity. For both Freud and Jung, multiplicity is basic to human nature, and their models of man rely upon a polycentric fantasy. Freud's notion of the child as sexually polymorphous originates the libido in a polymorphic, polyvalent, and polycentric field of erogenous zones. Jung's model of personality (q.v.) is essentially multiple, and Jung correlates the plurality of its archetypal structure with the polytheistic stage of culture (CW 9, ii, §427). Hence, "the soul's inherent multiplicity demands a theological fantasy of equal differentiation" (Hillman 1975a, p. 167).

(2) The tradition of thought (Greek, Renaissance, Romantic) to which archetypal psychology claims it is an heir is set in polytheistic attitudes. The imaginative products of these historical periods cannot contribute further to psychology unless the consciousness that would receive from them is able to transpose itself into a similar polytheistic framework. The high achievements of Western culture from which contemporary culture may find sources for its survival remain closed to modern consciousness unless it gains a perspective mimetic to what it is examining. Hence, polytheistic psychology is necessary for the continuity of culture.

(3) The social, political, and psychiatric critique implied throughout archetypal psychology mainly concerns the monotheistic hero-myth (now called ego-psychology) of secular humanism, i.e., the single-centered, self-identified notion of subjective consciousness of humanism (from Protagoras to Sartre). It is this myth which has dominated the soul and which leads to both unreflected action and self-blindness (Oedipus). It is responsible also for the repression of a psychological diversity that then appears as psychopathology. Hence, a polytheistic psychology is necessary for reawakening reflective consciousness and bringing a new reflection to psychopathology.

(4) The *perspectivalism* of archetypal psychology requires a deepening of subjectivity beyond mere Nietzschean perspectives or existential stances. Perspectives are *forms* of vision, rhetoric, values, epistemology, and lived styles that perdure independently of empirical individuality. For archetypal psychology, pluralism and multiplicity and relativism are not enough: these are merely philosophical generalities. Psychology needs to specify and differentiate each event, which it can do against the variegated background of archetypal configurations, or what polytheism called Gods, in order to make multiplicity both authentic and precise. Thus the question it asks of an event is not *why* or *how*, but rather *what* specifically is being presented and ultimately *who*, which divine figure, is speaking in this style of consciousness, this form of presentation. Hence, a polytheistic psychology is necessary for the authorization of "a pluralistic universe" (William James 1909), for consistencies within it, and for precision of its differentiation.

The polytheistic analogy is both religious and not religious (Miller 1972, 1974; Bregman 1980; Scott 1980; Avens 1980). The Gods are taken essentially, as foundations, so that psychology points beyond soul and can never be merely agnostic. The sacred and sacrificial dimension—the religious instinct as Jung calls it—is given a place of main value; and, in truth, it is precisely because of the appeal to the Gods that value enters the psychological field, creating claims on each human life and giving personal acts more than personal significance. The Gods are therefore the Gods of religion and not mere nomina, categories, devices ex machina. They are respected as powers and persons and creators of value.

A distinction is nonetheless maintained between polytheism as psychology and as religion. This distinction is difficult because "depth analysis leads to the soul which inevitably involves analysis in religion and even in theology, while at the same time living religion, experienced religion, originates in the human psyche and is as such a psychological phenomenon" (Hillman 1967a, p. 42). When soul is the first metaphor (q.v.), then psychology and religion must be inter-twined and their distinction arbitrary or ambiguous. The question of polytheism is posed by the soul itself as soon as its perspective experiences the world as animated and its own nature as replete with changing diversity. That is, as soon as the soul is freed from ego domination, the question of poly-theism arises.

Yet archetypal psychology is "not out to worship Greek Gods or those of any other polytheistic high culture. . . . We are not reviving a dead faith. For we are not concerned with faith" (Hillman 1975a, p. 170; cf. A. H. Armstrong 1981). The Gods of psychology are not believed in, not taken liter-ally, not imagined theologically. "Religion approaches Gods with ritual, prayer, sacrifice, worship, creed. . . . In arche-typal psychology, Gods are *imagined*. They are approached through psychological methods of personifying, pathologiz-ing, and psychologizing. They are formulated ambiguously, as metaphors for modes of experience and as numinous borderline persons. They are cosmic perspectives in which the soul participates" (ibid., p. 169). Mainly, the mode of this participation is reflection: the Gods are discovered in recognizing the stance of one's perspective, one's psychologi-cal sensitivity to the configurations that dominate one's styles of thought and life. Gods for psychology do not have to be experienced in direct mystical encounter or in effigies, whether as concrete figures or as theological definitions.

A saying attributed to Hegel declares: "what is required is a 'monotheism of reason and heart, a polytheism of imagina-tion and art'" (Cook 1973). Inasmuch as archetypal psychology is imaginative, it requires imaginative first principles and polytheism becomes necessary, although it definitely does not carry on the rationalist separation between heart and art, between valuative and aesthetic sensitivities.

The critique of theological religion continues that done by Freud and Jung, though with an even more radical cast. Archetypal psychology does not attempt to correct the Judeo-Christian religion as illusion (Freud) or transform it as one-sided (Jung). It shifts the ground of the entire question to a polytheistic position. In this single stroke, it carries out Freud's and Jung's critiques to their ultimate consequent —the death of God as a monotheistic fantasy, while at the same time restoring the fullness of the Gods in all things and, let it be said, reverting psychology itself to the recognition that it too is a religious activity (Hillman 1975a, p. 227). If a religious instinct is inherent to the psyche as Jung maintained, then any psychology attempting to do justice to the psyche must recognize its religious nature.

A polytheistic vision differs from undifferentiated pantheism, holy vitalism, and naturalistic animism—which from the standpoint of monotheistic consciousness tend to be bunched together as "pagan" and "primitive." Gods in archetypal psychology are not some primal energy suffused through the universe nor are they imagined to be independent magical powers working on us through things. Gods are imagined as the formal intelligibility of the phenomenal world, allowing each thing to be discerned for its inherent intelligibility and for its specific place of belonging to this or that *kosmos* (ordered pattern or arrangement). The Gods are *places*, and myths make place for psychic events that in an only human world become pathological. By offering shelter and altar, the Gods can order and make intelligible the entire phenomenal world of nature and human consciousness. All phenomena are 'saved' by the act of placing them which at once gives them value. We discover what belongs where by means of likeness, the analogy of events with mythical configurations. This mode was current during millennia of our culture in alchemy, planetary astrology, natural philosophy, and medicine, each of which studied the microcosmic things in rapport with macrocosmic Gods (Moore 1982; Boer 1980). It was this question of *placing* that was addressed to the Greek oracles: "To what gods or hero must I pray or sacrifice to achieve such and such a purpose?" If one knows where an event belongs, to whom it can be related, then one is able to proceed.

Today, however, the discovery of what belongs where, the *epistrophé* or reversion through likeness of an event to its mythical pattern, is less the aim of archetypal psychology than is an archetypal sensitivity that all things belong to myth. The study of these archetypal placings, deriving from the work of Frances Yates (1966) in regard to the Memory Theatre of the Florentine, Giulio Camillo (c. 1480–1544), has been carried out in some detail in seminars by Lopez-Pedraza and by Sardello.

11   Psychopathology

The point of departure for the re-visioning of psychopathology is a statement from Jung (1929, CW 13, §54): "The gods have become diseases; Zeus no longer rules Olympus but rather the solar plexus, and produces curious specimens for the doctor's consulting room. . . . "

The link between Gods and diseases is double: on the one hand, giving the dignity of archetypal significance and divine reflection to every symptom whatsoever, and on the other hand, suggesting that myth and its figures may be examined for patterns of pathology. Hillman (1974a) has called this pathology in mythical figures the *infirmitas* of the archetype, by which is meant both the essential "infirmity" of all archetypal forms—that they are not perfect, not transcendent, not idealizations—and that they therefore provide "nursing" to human conditions; they are the embracing backgrounds within which our personal sufferings can find support and be cared for.

The double link—that pathology is mythologized and mythology is pathologized—had already been adumbrated by Freud's presentation of the Oedipus myth as the key to the pathology of neurosis and even of the civilization as a whole. Before Freud, the link between *mythos* and *pathos* can be discovered in Nietzsche's *Birth of Tragedy* and in the scholarly research of the great German classicist and encyclopaedist, Wilhelm Heinrich Roscher, whose *Ephialtes* (1900), a monograph on Pan and the Nightmare, was subtitled "A Mythopathological Study" (cf. Hillman 1972a).

The relations between myths and psychopathology are elaborated in a series of studies: Lopez-Pedraza (1977) on Hermes and (1982) on the Titans; Berry (1975) on Demeter/Persephone and (1979b) on Echo; Moore (1979a) on Artemis; Micklem (1979) on Medusa; Hillman (1970a, 1975d) on Saturn, (1974a) on Athene and Ananke, (1972c) on Eros and on Dionysus, (1972a) on Pan, and (1967b) on the puer eternus or divinely youthful figure in various mythologies; M. Stein (1973) on Hephaistos and (1977) on Hera. In these studies, the myth is examined for its pathological implications. The hermeneutic begins with myths and mythical figures (not with a case), reading them downward for psychological understanding of the fantasies going on in behavior.

Thereby archetypal psychology follows the epistrophic (reversion) method of Corbin, returning to the higher principle in order to find place for and understand the lesser—the images before their examples. Imagination becomes a *method* for investigating and comprehending psychopathology. This hermeneutic method is also essentially Neoplatonic; it is the preferred way for deciphering the grotesque and pathologized configurations of Renaissance psychology. As Wind says in his "Observation on Method" (1967, p. 238): "The commonplace may be understood as a reduction of the exceptional, but the exceptional cannot be understood by amplifying the commonplace. Both logically and causally the exceptional is crucial, because it introduces . . . the more comprehensive category."

Precisely because myth presents the exceptional, the outlandish, and more-than-human dimension, it offers background to the sufferings of souls *in extremis*, i.e., what nineteenth-century medicine calls 'psychopathology.' The double movement between pathology and mythology moreover implies that the pathological is always going on in human life inasmuch as life enacts mythical fantasies. Archetypal psychology further claims that it is mainly through the wounds in human life that the Gods enter (rather than through pronouncedly sacred or mystical events), because pathology is the most palpable manner of bearing witness to the powers beyond ego control and the insufficiency of the ego perspective.

This perpetually recurring "pathologizing" is defined as "the psyche's autonomous ability to create illness, morbidity, disorder, abnormality, and suffering in any aspect of its behavior and to experience and imagine life through this deformed and afflicted perspective" (Hillman 1975a, p. 57). There is no cure of pathologizing; there is, instead, a re-evaluation.

That pathologizing is also a "deformed perspective" accounts for its place in the work of imagination which, according to Gaston Bachelard (1884–1962)—another major source of the archetypal tradition—must proceed by "deforming the images offered by perception" (Bachelard 1943, p. 7). It is this pathologized eye which, like that of the artist and the psychoanalyst, prevents the phenomena of the soul from being naively understood as merely natural. Following Jung (and his research into alchemy), psychological work is an *opus contra naturam*. This idea Hillman (1975a, pp. 84–96) follows further by attacking the "naturalistic fallacy" which dominates most normative psychologies.

Another direction of the *mythos/pathos* connection starts with one specific form of pathology, searching it for its mythical possibilities, as if to uncover "the God in the disease." Examples are: Lockhart (1977) cancer; Moore (1979b) asthma; Leveranz (1979) epilepsy; Hawkins (1979) migraine; Severson (1979) skin disorders; Kugelmann, glaucoma; Sipiora (1981) tuberculosis.

There are also more general reflections upon pathology re-visioned within an archetypal hermeneutic: R. Stein (1974) on psychosexual disorders; Guggenbühl-Craig (1971) on the archetypal power problem in medical attitudes; Ziegler (1980) on archetypal medicine; Sardello (1980a) on medicine, disease, and the body. These works look at the body, pathology, and its treatment altogether free from the positivism of the clinical and empirical traditions that have come down to the twentieth century from nineteenth-century scientistic, materialistic medicine, its views of health, disease, and the power-hero role of the physician.

In one respect, the position here is close to the anti-psychiatry of Thomas Szasz and R. D. Laing. Each regards 'abnormal' conditions as existentially human and hence fundamentally normal. They become psychiatric conditions when looked at psychiatrically. Archetypal psychology, however, makes three further moves beyond anti-psychiatry. First, it examines the normalizing perspective itself in order to show its 'abnormalities' and pathologizing propensities. Second, unlike Szasz and Laing, archetypal psychology maintains the real existence of psychopathology as such, as inherent to psychic reality. It neither denies psychopathology nor attempts to find cause for it outside the soul in politics, professional power, or social convention. Third, because pathologizing is inherent to psyche, it is also necessary. The necessity of pathologizing derives, on the one hand, from the Gods who show patterns of psychopathology and, on the other hand, from the soul which becomes aware of its destiny in death mainly through the psyche's indefatigable and amazingly inventive capacity to pathologize.

As Freud's paradigm of psychopathology was hysteria (and paranoia) and Jung's was schizophrenia, archetypal psychology has so far spoken mainly about depression (Hillman 1972c, 1975a, c, d, 1979a; Vitale 1973; Berry 1975, 1978b; Guggenbühl-Craig 1979; Miller 1981b; Simmer 1981) and mood disorder (Sardello 1980b). Depression has also provided a focus for *Kulturkritik*, an attack upon social and medical conventions that do not allow the vertical depth of depressions.

For, a society that does not allow its individuals "to go down" cannot find its depth and must remain permanently inflated in a manic mood disorder disguised as 'growth.' Hillman (1975a, p. 98) links the Western horror of depression with the tradition of the heroic ego and Christian salvation through upward resurrection. "Depression is still the Great Enemy. . . . Yet through depression we enter depths and in depths find soul. Depression is essential to the tragic sense of life. It moistens the dry soul and dries the wet. It brings refuge, limitation, focus, gravity, weight, and humble powerlessness. It reminds of death. The true revolution (in behalf of soul) begins in the individual who can be true to his or her depression."

12   *The Practice of Therapy*

Archetypal psychology continues the ritual procedures of classical analysis deriving from Freud and Jung: (1) regular meetings (2) with individual patients (3) face-to-face (4) at the therapist's locus (5) for a fee. (Groups, couples, and children are generally eschewed; minor attention is paid to diagnostic and typological categories and to psychological testing.) These five procedures, however, are not rigid, and any of them may be modified or abandoned. Classical analysis (Hillman 1975b, p. 101) has been defined as: "a course of treatment in an atmosphere of sympathy and confidence of one person by another person for a fee, which treatment may be conceived as educative in various senses or therapeutic in various senses and which proceeds principally through the joint interpretative exploration of habitual behavior and of classes of mental events that have been traditionally called fantasies, feelings, memories, dreams and ideas, and where the exploration follows a coherent set of methods, concepts and beliefs stemming mainly from Freud and from Jung, where focus is preferably upon the unanticipated and affectively charged, and whose goal is the improvement (subjectively and/or objectively determined) of the analysand and the termination of the treatment."

If analysis "terminates," then it is governed by linear time. Casey (1979, p. 157) exposes this assumption: ". . . the time of soul is not to be presumed continuous. . . . it is discontinuous, not simply as having breaks or gaps . . . but as having many avatars, many kinds and modes. The polycentricity of the psyche demands no less than this, namely, a polyform time. . . ." That analyses have been growing longer since the early years with Freud and Jung must be understood as a phenomenon of the soul's temporality: "It is the soul, after all, that is taking all this extra time, and it must be doing so for reasons of its own which have primarily to do with . . . taking more world-time so as to encourage the efflorescence of its own imaginal time" (ibid., p. 156).

Practice is rooted in Jung's view of the psyche as inherently purposeful: all psychic events whatsoever have *telos*. Archetypal psychology, however, does not enunciate this telos. Purposefulness qualifies psychic events, but it is not to be literalized apart from the images in which it inheres. Thus archetypal psychology refrains from stating goals for therapy (individuation or wholeness) and for its phenomena such as symptoms and dreams (compensations, warnings, prophetic indications). Purpose remains a *perspective* toward events in Jung's original description of the prospective versus the reductive view. Positive formulations of the telos of analysis lead only into teleology and dogmas of goals. Archetypal psychology fosters the sense of purpose as therapeutic in itself because it enhances the patient's interest in psychic phenomena, including the most objectionable symptoms, as intentional. But the therapist does not literalize these intentions, and therefore therapy follows the Freudian mode of restraint and abstention. It moves along a *via negativa*, attempting to deliteralize all formulations of purpose so that the analysis is reduced to sticking with the actual images.

The specific focus and atmosphere of archetypal psychology's way of working and further departures from classical analysis must be culled from many publications for two reasons: there is no program of training (no didactic), and no single work lays out the theory of the practice of therapy. (Publications particularly relevant are: Guggenbühl-Craig 1970, 1971, 1972, 1979; Berry 1978a, 1981; Hillman and Berry 1977; Grinnell 1973; Frey, Bosnak et al. 1978; Giegerich 1977; Hillman 1975a, 1972a, 1964, 1977b, c, 1975c, 1974a; Hartman 1980; Newman 1980; Watkins 1981.)

Departures from classical analysis lie less in the form of therapy than in its focus. Archetypal psychology conceives therapy, as it does psychopathology, as the enactment of fantasy. Rather than prescribe or employ therapy for pathology, it self-examines the fantasy of therapy (so that therapy does not perpetuate the literal pathology which calls therapy forth and is called forth by a literal therapy). Archetypal psychology seeks to remind therapy of its notions of itself (Giegerich 1977), attempting to lift repression from the unconsciousness of therapy itself.

In "The Fiction of Case History," Hillman (1975c) examines the case model used by Freud, and by analysts ever since, as a style of narrative. At once, the problem of cases and the problems told by cases become the subject of an imaginative, literary reflection of which the clinical is only one genre. Genres or categories of the literary imagination —epic, detective, comic, social realist, picaresque—become relevant for understanding the organization of narratives told in therapy. Since "the way we tell our story is the way

we form our therapy" (Berry 1974, p. 69), the entire procedure of therapeutic work must be reconceived in terms of
the poetic basis of mind. An essential work of therapy is to
become conscious of the fictions in which the patient is cast
and to re-write or ghost-write, collaboratively, the story by
re-telling it in a more profound and authentic style. In this
re-told version in which imaginative art becomes the model,
the personal failures and sufferings of the patient are essential
to the story as they are to art.

The *explication du text* (with which the examination in
therapy of images and narrative details can be compared)
derives in part from the "personal construct theory" (1955) of
George Kelly (1905–1966). Experience is never raw or brute;
it is always constructed by images which are revealed in the
patient's narrations. The fantasy in which a problem is set
tells more about the way the problem is constructed and how
it can be transformed (reconstructed) than does any attempt
at analyzing the problem in its own terms.

A paper presented by Hillman and Berry at the First International Seminar of Archetypal Psychology (January 1977)
declares: "Ours could be called an *image-focused therapy*.
Thus the dream as an image or bundle of images is paradig-
matic, as if we were placing the entire psychotherapeutic procedure within the context of a dream" (cf. Berry 1974, 1978a,
and Hillman 1977b, 1978a, 1979a, b, for method and examples of dream work). It is not, however, that dreams as
such become the focus of therapy but that all events are
regarded from a dream-viewpoint, as if they were images,
metaphorical expressions. The dream is not in the patient
and something he or she does or makes; the patient is in the
dream and is doing or being made by its fiction. These same
papers on dream work exhibit how an image can be created,
that is, how an event can be heard as metaphor through

various manipulations: grammatical reversals, removal of punctuation, restatement and echo, humor, amplification. The aim of working with dreams or life events as dreams is to bring reflection to declarative and unreflected discourse, so that words no longer believe they refer to objective referents; instead, speech becomes imagistic, self-referent, descriptive of a psychic condition as its very expression (Berry 1982).

The detailed examination of presentational images— whether from dreams, from life situations, or the waking imagination of fantasy—has been a subject for Watkins (1976); Garufi (1977); Humbert (1971); Berry (1979a, b); Hillman (1977a, c). Here the work is a further refinement of Jung's technique of "active imagination" (Hull 1971).

Active imagination at times becomes the method of choice in therapy. There is direct perception of and engagement with an imaginary figure or figures. These figures with whom one converses or performs actions or which one depicts plastically are not conceived to be merely internal projections or only parts of the personality (q.v.). They are given the respect and dignity due independent beings. They are imagined seriously, though *not literally*. Rather like Neoplatonic *daimones*, and like angels in Corbin's sense, their 'between' reality is neither physical nor metaphysical, although just "as real as you—as a psychic entity—are real" (Jung, CW 14, §753). This development of true imaginative power (the *vera imaginatio* of Paracelsus; the *himma* of the heart of Corbin) and the ability to live one's life in the company of ghosts, familiars, ancestors, guides—the populace of the metaxy—are also aims of an archetypal therapy (Hillman 1977c, 1979c).

Recently, image-focused therapy has extended into the sensate world of perceptual objects and habitual forms —buildings, bureaucratic systems, conventional language, transportation, urban environment, food, education. This project has no less an ambition than the recuperation of the *anima mundi* or soul of the world by scrutinizing the face of the world as aesthetic physiognomy. This move envisages therapy altogether beyond the encounter of two persons in private and takes on the larger task of re-imagining the public world within which the patient lives (Ogilvy 1977). This notion of therapy attempts to realize the poetic basis of mind in actuality, as an imaginative, aesthetic response. When the environment is recognized as imagistic, then each person reacts to it in a more psychological manner, thereby extending both the notion of the 'psychological' to the aesthetic and the notion of therapy from occasional hours in the consulting room to a continual imaginative activity in the home, the street, while eating, or watching television.

Feeling

The liberation of therapy from the exclusivity of the consulting room first requires a re-evaluation of the identity psyche = feeling, that identification of the individual with emotion which has characterized all schools of psychotherapy ever since Freud's work with conversion hysteria, emotional abreaction, and transference. In brief, therapy has been concerned with personal feeling, and the patient's images have been reduced to his feelings. Hillman (1960, 1971), in two books devoted to emotion and to feeling, began a phenomenological and differentiated analysis of the notions and theories of feeling and emotion as an avenue toward releasing therapy, and psychology itself, from the inevitable narrowing into personalism occasioned by the identification of soul with feeling. The main argument against the personal confessional mode of therapy (Hillman 1979c)—besides its perpetuating the Cartesian division of ensouled subject/lifeless object—is that it fosters the delusion of ownership of emotion, as belonging to the proprium (Allport 1955). The intensified singleness that emotions bring, their narrowing monocentristic effect upon consciousness, gives support to the already monotheistic tendency of the ego to appropriate and identify with its experiences. Emotions reinforce ego psychology. Moreover, when emotion and feeling are conceived as primary, images must play a secondary role. They are considered to be derivative and descriptive of feelings.

Instead, archetypal psychology reverses the relation of feeling and image: feelings are considered to be, as William Blake said, "divine influxes," accompanying, qualifying, and energizing images. They are not merely personal but belong to imaginal reality, the reality of the image, and help make the image felt as a specific value. Feelings elaborate its complexity, and feelings are as complex as the image that contains them. Not images represent feelings, but feelings are inherent to images. Berry (1974, p. 63) writes: "A dream image is or has the quality of emotion. . . . They [emotions] adhere or inhere to the image and may not be explicit at all. . . . We cannot entertain any image in dreams, or poetry or painting, without experiencing an emotional quality presented by the image itself." This further implies that any event experienced as an image is at once animated, emotionalized, and placed in the realm of value.

The task of therapy is to return personal feelings (anxiety, desire, confusion, boredom, misery) to the specific images which hold them. Therapy attempts to individualize the face of each emotion: the body of desire, the face of fear, the situation of despair. Feelings are imagined into their details. This move is similar to that of the imagist theory of poetry (Hulme

1924), where any emotion not differentiated by a specific image is inchoate, common, and dumb, remaining both sentimentally personal and yet collectively unindividualized.

13   *Eros*

Since its inception, depth psychology has consistently recognized the special role of eros in its work. In fact, psychoanalysis has been as much an eroto-analysis as an analysis of soul, since its basic perspective toward soul has been libidinal. The omnipresence of eros in therapy and in the theory of all depth psychologies receives this recognition under the technical term transference.

Archetypal psychology, analogously to Jung's alchemical psychology of transference, imagines transference against a mythical background—the Eros and Psyche mythologem from Apuleius's *Golden Ass* (Hillman 1972c, pp. 63–125)— thereby de-historicizing and de-personalizing the phenomenology of love in therapy as well as in any human passion. "By recognizing the primacy of the image, archetypal thought frees both psyche and logos to an Eros that is imaginal" (Bedford 1981, p. 245). The imaginal, mythical transposition implies that all erotic phenomena whatsoever, including erotic symptoms, seek psychological consciousness and that all psychic phenomena whatsoever, including neurotic and psychotic symptoms, seek erotic embrace. Wherever psyche is the subject of endeavor or the perspective taken toward events, erotic entanglements will necessarily occur because the mythological tandem necessitates their appearance together. While Apuleius's myth details the obstacles in the relation between love and soul, R. Stein (1974) has developed an archetypal approach to the incestuous family hindrances which prevent eros from becoming psychological and psyche from becoming erotic.

The idea of a mythic tandem as basis of transference was first suggested by Freud's Oedipal theory and elaborated by Jung in his anima/animus theory (*CW* 16). Archetypal psychology has gone on to describe a variety of tandems: Senex and Puer (Hillman 1967b); Venus and Vulcan (M. Stein 1973); Pan and the Nymphs (Hillman 1972a); Apollo and Daphne; Apollo and Dionysus; Hermes and Apollo (Lopez-Pedraza 1977); Zeus and Hera (M. Stein 1977); Artemis and Puer (Moore 1979a); Echo and Narcissus (Berry 1979b); Demeter and Persephone (Berry 1975); Mother and Son (Hillman 1973b). Guggenbühl-Craig has discussed the archetypal fantasies operating in the patient-helper relationship (1971) and in the dyad of marriage (1977). These tandems provide occasion for the examination of diverse forms of erotic relationships, their rhetorics and expectations, the particular styles of suffering, and the interlocking mutualities that each tandem imposes. These tandems are imagined also as going on intra-psychically, as patterns of relations between complexes within an individual.

Since love of soul is also love of image, archetypal psychology considers transference, including its strongest sexualized demonstrations, to be a phenomenon of imagination. Nowhere does the impersonality of myth strike a human life more personally. Thus transference is the paradigm for working through the relations of personal and literal with the impersonal and imaginal. Transference is thus nothing less than the eros required by the awakening of psychic reality; and this awakening imposes archetypal roles upon patient and therapist, not the least of which is that of "psychological patient" which means one who suffers or is impassioned by psyche. For this erotic—not medical—reason, archetypal psychology retains the term "patient" instead of client, analysand, trainee, etc. The erotic struggles in any relationship are also psychological struggles with images, and as this *psychomachia* proceeds in an archetypal therapy, there is a transformation of love from a repression and/or obsession with images to a slow love of them, to a recognition that love is itself rooted in images, their continuous creative appearance and their love for that particular human soul in which they manifest.

14   *Personality Theory: Personifying*

Archetypal psychology's personality theory differs fundamentally from the main views of personality in Western psychology. If pathologizing belongs to the soul and is not to be combated by a strong ego, and if therapy (q.v.) consists in giving support to the counter-ego forces, the personified figures who are ego-alien, then both the theory of psychopathology and that of therapy assume a personality theory that is not ego-centered.

The first axiom of this theory is based on the late development of Jung's complex theory (1946) which holds that every personality is essentially multiple (CW 8, §388ff.). Multiple personality is humanity in its natural condition. In other cultures these multiple personalities have names, locations, energies, functions, voices, angel and animal forms, and even theoretical formulations as different kinds of soul. In our culture the multiplicity of personality is regarded either as a psychiatric aberration or, at best, as unintegrated introjections or partial personalities. The psychiatric fear of multiple personality indicates the identification of personality with a partial capacity, the 'ego,' which is in turn the psychological enactment of a two-thousand-year monotheistic tradition that has elevated unity over multiplicity.

Archetypal psychology extends Jung's personified naming of the components of personality—shadow, anima, animus, trickster, old wise man, great mother, etc. "Personifying or imagining things" (Hillman 1975a, pp. 1–51) becomes crucial for moving from an abstract, objectified psychology to one that encourages animistic engagement with the world. Personifying further allows the multiciplicity of psychic phenomena to be experienced as voices, faces, and names. Psychic phenomena can then be perceived with precision and particularity, rather than generalized in the manner of faculty psychology as feelings, ideas, sensations, and the like.

For archetypal psychology, consciousness is given with the various 'partial' personalities. Rather than being imagined as split-off fragments of the 'I,' they are better reverted to the differentiated models of earlier psychologies where the complexes would have been called souls, daimones, genii, and other mythical-imaginal figures. The consciousness that is postulated a priori with these figures or personifications is demonstrated by their interventions in ego control, i.e., the psychopathology of everyday life (Freud), disturbances of attention in the association experiments (Jung), the willfulness and aims of figures in dreams, the obsessive moods and compulsive thoughts that may intrude during any *abaissment du niveau mental* (Janet). Whereas most psychologies attempt to ban these personalities as disintegrative, archetypal psychology favors bringing non-ego figures to further awareness and considers this tension with the non-ego which relativizes the ego's surety and single perspective to be a chief occupation of soul-making (q.v.).

Thus, personality is conceived less in terms of stages in life and development, of typologies of character and functioning, of psycho-energetics toward goals (social, individual, etc.) or of faculties (will, affect, reason) and their balance. Rather, personality is imaginatively conceived as a living and peopled drama in which the subject 'I' takes part but is neither the sole author, nor director, nor always the main character. Sometimes he or she is not even on the stage. At other times, the other theories of personality just reviewed may play their parts as necessary fictions for the drama.

The healthy or mature or ideal personality will thus show cognizance of its dramatically masked and ambiguous situation. Irony, humor, and compassion will be its hallmarks, since these traits bespeak an awareness of the multiplicity of meanings and fates and the multiplicity of intentions embodied by any subject at any moment. The 'healthy personality' is imagined less upon a model of natural, primitive, or ancient man with its nostalgia, or upon social-political man with its mission, or bourgeois rational man with its moralism, but instead against the background of artistic man for whom imagining is a style of living and whose reactions are reflexive, animal, immediate. This model is, of course, not meant literally or singly. It serves to stress certain values of personality to which archetypal psychology gives importance: sophistication, complexity, and impersonal profundity; an animal flow with life disregarding concepts of will, choice, and decision; morality as dedication to crafting the soul (soul-making, q.v.); sensitivity to traditional continuities; the significance of pathologizing and living at the 'borders'; aesthetic responsiveness.

15   *Biographical*

As shown above, archetypal psychology is not a theoretical system emanating from the thought of one person for whom it is named, then identifying with a small group, becoming a school, and moving into the world in the manner of Freudian or Jungian psychologies; nor does it emerge from a particular clinic, laboratory, or city giving it its name. Rather, archetypal psychology presents the polytheistic structure of a post-modern consciousness. It is a style of thinking, a fashion of mind, a revisionist engagement on many fronts: therapy, education, literary criticism, medicine, philosophy, and the material world. It assembles and lends its terms and viewpoints to a variety of intellectual concerns in contemporary thought. Eros (q.v.) and a common concern for soul, image, and pathology draw individuals from diverse geographical and intellectual areas into rapport with each other for the re-visioning of their ideas and their worlds.

Inasmuch as the sources (q.v.) are in Jung and Corbin, the biographical origins can be traced to the Eranos Conferences at Ascona, Switzerland (Rudolf Ritsema), where Jung and Corbin were perennially major speakers; Durand and Hillman entered that circle in the 1960s, Miller in the 1970s, and Giegerich in 1982. The Platonist inspiration at Eranos, its concern for spirit in a time of crisis and decay, the mutuality of engagement that transcends academic specialization, and the educative effect of eros on soul were together formative in the directions that archetypal psychology was subsequently to take.

A second biographical strand can be discerned in a period (April 1969) at the Warburg Institute in London and the confrontation by Lopez-Pedraza, Hillman, and Berry with the tradition of classical (pagan, polytheistic) images in the Western psyche. Here they found witness to a ground for psychology in the cultural imagination, especially of the Mediterranean, which would allow psychology to return from its distractions by natural science and Eastern spirituality. Third was the re-founding (1970) in Zürich of the formerly Jungian journal *Spring* as an organ of archetypal thought and the launching of other publications, as well as seminars on psychological readings of Renaissance images.

Fourth, subsequent developments took place in the Western Hemisphere. In February 1972 the invitation to give the distinguished Dwight Harrington Terry Lectures at Yale University enabled Hillman (1975a) to present the first comprehensive formulation of archetypal psychology. This was followed by the appointment of Hillman and Berry as visiting lecturers in the Yale psychology faculty, where their association with the Yale philosopher Edward Casey turned their work toward mutual explorations of the philosophy of imagination and phenomenology. During the mid-seventies, graduate degree programs were being established at Sonoma State, California (Gordon Tappan), and the University of Dallas (Robert Sardello). In 1976 Hillman and Berry joined the faculty of the Department of Religions at Syracuse University, New York, and in collaboration with David Miller worked further into the problems of monotheistic and polytheistic thinking. In January 1977, partly sponsored by a grant from the Rockefeller Brothers Foundation, archetypal psychology held its first International Seminar at the University of Dallas, gathering together some twenty of the individuals mentioned in this article. Other conferences and seminars were held at the University of Notre Dame, Indiana

(Thomas Kapacinskas), Duquesne University, Pennsylvania, and the University of New Mexico (Howard McConeghey). In January 1978, the University of Dallas appointed Hillman Professor of Psychology and Senior Fellow in the Institute of Philosophic Studies (Robert Sardello) and Berry as Visiting Professor.

Meanwhile, Lopez-Pedraza had been appointed Lecturer in mythology and psychology in the Faculty of Letters at the University of Caracas. With the opening (1981) of the Dallas Institute of Humanities and Culture (whose Fellows include Sardello, Thomas, Moore, Stroud, Berry, Hillman, and Guggenbühl-Craig), archetypal psychology turned toward the 'soul in the world' *(anima mundi)* of the city. 'City' becomes the patient, the place of pathologizing, and the locus where the soul's imagination is actualized on earth, requiring an archetypally psychological perspective for examining its ills.

No nation in Europe has responded more attentively to this re-visionist thought than Italy. A number of engaged intellectuals and therapists in Rome, Florence, Pisa, and Milan have succeeded in translating (Aldo Giuliani) works of archetypal psychology in the *Rivista di psicologia analitica*, in books (Adelphi, Communitá), and in publications of the *Enciclopedia Italiana* and have presented its thought in teaching, editing, and translating (Francesco Donfrancesco, Bianca Garufi). In France, a similar initiative, joining with the groups affiliated with Corbin and Durand, was pioneered by Editions Imago, by Michel Cazenave and by Monique Salzmann.

Two recent European events—a world conference in Cordoba on "Science and Consciousness" (Cazenave 1980), reflecting the thought of Jung and Corbin and the Eranos circle (Miller, Izutsu, Durand, Raine, Hillman) in relation with contemporary physical sciences, and an address by Hillman (1982) on archetypal psychology as a Renaissance psychology in Florence (Donfrancesco)—have presented what is reviewed in this essay in the wide current of contemporary Western ideas.

Part Two

References

Nota bene: All references to *Spring: An Annual of Archetypal Psychology and Jungian Thought* have been given by year and pages; the publisher is Spring Publications, at times located in New York, Zürich, Irving, Texas, and Dallas. Within the text, all references to C. G. Jung follow the standard abbreviation of his *Collected Works* (*CW*, volume number, paragraph number), published by Princeton University Press and by Routledge and Kegan Paul, London. Each bibliography entry includes after the author's name the date that appears in the text when that source is cited.

Allport, Gordon (1955). *Becoming* (The Terry Lectures). New Haven: Yale University Press, 1955.

Armstrong, A. H. (1981). "Some Advantages of Polytheism." *Dionysius* 5 (1981): 181–88.

Armstrong, Robert P. (1971). *The Affecting Presence.* Urbana: University of Illinois Press, 1971.

Avens, Roberts (1980). *Imagination Is Reality: Western Nirvana in Jung, Hillman, Barfield and Cassirer.* Spring Publications, 1980.

——— (1982a). "Heidegger and Archetypal Psychology." *International Philosophical Quarterly* 22 (1982): 183–202.

—— (1982b). *Imaginal Body: Para-Jungian Reflections on Soul, Imagination and Death.* Washington, D. C.: University Press of America, 1982.

Bachelard, Gaston (1943). *L'Air et les songes.* Paris: Corti, 1943.

Bedford, Gary S. (1981). "Notes on Mythological Psychology." *Journal of the American Academy of Religion* 49 (1981): 231–47.

*Berry, Patricia (1973). "On Reduction." *Spring 1973:* 67–84.

—— (1974). "An Approach to the Dream." *Spring 1974:* 58–79.

—— (1975). "The Rape of Demeter/Persephone and Neurosis." *Spring 1975:* 186–98.

—— (1978a). "Defense and Telos in Dreams." *Spring 1978:* 115–27.

—— (1978b). *What's the Matter with Mother?* Pamphlet, London: Guild of Pastoral Psychology, 1978.

—— (1979a). "Virginities of Image." Paper: *Dragonflies* Conference on Virginity in Psyche, Myth, and Community, University of Dallas, 1979.

—— (1979b). "Echo's Passion." Paper: *Dragonflies* Conference on Beauty in Psyche, Myth, and Community, University of Dallas, 1979.

—— (1981). "The training of shadow and the shadow of training." *Journal of Analytical Psychology* 26 (1981): 221–28.

—— (1982). "Hamlet's Poisoned Ear." *Spring 1982:* 195–210.

Boer, Charles, trans. (1980). *Marsilio Ficino: The Book of Life.* Spring Publications, 1980.

*The papers of Patricia Berry have subsequently been collected in one volume, *Echo's Subtle Body*, Dallas: Spring Publications, 1982.

—— and Kugler, Peter (1977). "Archetypal Psychology Is Mythical Realism." *Spring 1977*: 131–52.

Bregman, Lucy (1980). "Religious Imagination: Polytheistic Psychology Confronts Calvin." *Soundings* 63 (1980): 36–60.

Casey, Edward S. (1974). "Toward an Archetypal Imagination." *Spring 1974*: 1–32.

—— (1976). *Imagining: A Phenomenological Study*. Bloomington: University of Indiana Press, 1976.

—— (1979). "Time in the Soul." *Spring 1979*: 144–64.

—— (1982). "Getting Placed: Soul in Space." *Spring 1982*: 1–25.

Cazenave, Michel (1980). *Science et Conscience*. Paris: Stock, 1980.

Christou, Evangelos (1963). *The Logos of the Soul*. Spring Publications, 1963.

Cook, Daniel J. (1973). *Language in the Philosophy of Hegel*, p. 62. The Hague: Mouton, 1973.

Corbin, Henry (1958). *L'Imagination créatrice dans le Soufisme d'Ibn 'Arabi*. Paris: Flammarion, 1958 [in translation: *Creative Imagination in the Sufism of Ibn 'Arabi*. Bollingen Series, vol. 91. Princeton: Princeton University Press, 1969].

—— (1971–73). *En Islam iranien*. 4 vols. Paris: Gallimard, 1971–73.

—— (1977). *Spiritual Body and Celestial Earth*. Bollingen Series. Princeton: Princeton University Press, 1977.

—— (1979). *Avicenne et le récit visionnaire*. Paris: Berg International, 2d ed., 1979 [in translation: *Avicenna and the Visionary Recital*. Spring Publications, 1980].

Cowan, Lyn (1979). "On Masochism." *Spring 1979*: 42–54.

Durand, Gilbert (1960). *Les Structures anthropologiques de l'imaginaire: introduction á l'archétypologie générale.* Paris: Bordas, 6th ed., 1979.

—— (1975). *Science de l'homme et tradition.* Paris: Berg International, 1975.

—— (1979). *Figures mythiques et visages de l'oeuvre.* Paris: Berg International, 1979.

Frey-Wehrlin, C. T., Bosnak, R. et al. (1978). "The Treatment of Chronic Psychosis." *Journal of Analytical Psychology* 23 (1978): 253–57.

Garufi, Bianca (1977). "Reflections on the 'rêve éveillé dirigé' method." *Journal of Analytical Psychology* 22 (1977): 207–29.

Giegerich, Wolfgang (1977). "On the Neurosis of Psychology." *Spring 1977*: 153–74.

—— (1982). "Busse für Philemon: Vertiefung in das verdorbene Gast-Spiel der Götter." In *Eranos Jahrbuch 51—1982* (forthcoming).

Goldenberg, Naomi (1975). "Archetypal Theory after Jung." *Spring 1975*: 199–220.

—— (1979). *Changing of the Gods: Feminism and the End of Traditional Religion.* Boston: Beacon, 1979.

Grinnell, Robert (1973). *Alchemy in a Modern Woman.* Spring Publications, 1973.

Guggenbühl-Craig, Adolf (1970). "Must Analysis Fail through Its Destructive Aspect?" *Spring 1970*: 133–45.

—— (1971). *Macht als Gefahr beim Helfer.* Basel: Karger, 1971 [in translation: *Power in the Helping Professions.* Spring Publications, 1971].

—— (1972). "Analytical Rigidity and Ritual." *Spring 1972*: 34–42.

—— (1977). *Marriage—Dead or Alive*. Spring Publications, 1977.

—— (1979). "The Archetype of the Invalid and the Limits of Healing." *Spring 1979*: 29-41.

Hartman, Gary V. (1980). "Psychotherapy: An Attempt at Definition." *Spring 1980*: 90-100.

Hawkins, Ernest (1979). "On Migraine—From Dionysos to Freud." *Dragonflies: Studies in Imaginal Psychology* 1 (1979): 46-69.

Hillman, James (1960). *Emotion: A comprehensive phenomenology of theories and their meanings for therapy*. London: Routledge & Kegan Paul, 1960.

—— (1964). *Suicide and the Soul*. New York: Harper & Row, 1964 [reprinted: Spring Publications, 1976].

—— (1967a). *Insearch: Psychology and Religion*. London: Hodder and Stoughton, 1967 [reprinted: Spring Publications, 1979].

—— (1967b). "Senex and Puer." In *Puer Papers*, pp. 3-53. Spring Publications, 1979.

—— (1970a). "On Senex Consciousness." *Spring 1970*: 146-65.

—— (1970b). "Why 'Archetypal' Psychology?" *Spring 1970*: 212-19.

—— (1971). "The Feeling Function." In *Lectures on Jung's Typology* (with M.-L. von Franz), pp. 74-150. Spring Publications, 1971.

—— (1972a). "An Essay on Pan." In *Pan and the Nightmare* (with W. H. Roscher), pp. i-lxiii. Spring Publications, 1972.

—— (1972b). "Failure and Analysis." *Journal of Analytical Psychology* 17 (1972): 1-6.

—— (1972c). *The Myth of Analysis*. Evanston: North-western University Press, 1972.

—— (1973a). "Plotino, Ficino e Vico precursori della psicologia degli archetipi." *Rivista di Psicologia Analitica* 4 (1973): 322–40.

—— (1973b). "The Great Mother, Her Son, Her Hero, and the Puer." In *Fathers and Mothers: Five Papers on the Archetypal Background of Family Psychology*, edited by Patricia Berry, pp. 75–127. Spring Publications, 1973.

—— (1973c). "Anima." *Spring 1973*: 97–132.

—— (1974a). "On the Necessity of Abnormal Psychology." In *Eranos Jahrbuch 43—1974*, pp. 91–135. Leiden: E. J. Brill, 1977.

—— (1974b). "'Anima' (II)." *Spring 1974*: 113–46.

—— (1975a). *Re-Visioning Psychology*. New York: Harper & Row, 1975.

—— (1975b). *Loose Ends: Primary Papers in Archetypal Psychology*. Spring Publications, 1975.

—— (1975c). "The Fiction of Case History." In *Religion as Story*, edited by J. B. Wiggins, pp. 123–73. New York: Harper & Row, 1975.

—— (1975d). "The 'Negative' Senex and a Renaissance Solution." *Spring 1975*: 77–109.

—— (1976). "Peaks and Vales: The Soul/Spirit Distinction as Basis for the Differences between Psychotherapy and Spiritual Discipline." In *On the Way to Self-Knowledge*, edited by J. Needleman and D. Lewis, pp. 114–47. New York: Knopf, 1976 [reprinted: in *Puer Papers*, pp. 54–74. Spring Publications, 1979].

—— (1977a). "The Pandaemonium of Images: C. G. Jung's Contribution to *Know Thyself*." *New Lugano Review* 3 (1977): 35–45.

—— (1977b). "An Inquiry into Image." *Spring 1977*: 62–88.

—— (1977c). "Psychotherapy's Inferiority Complex." In *Eranos Jahrbuch 46—1977*, pp. 121–74. Frankfurt a/M: Insel Verlag, 1981.

—— (1978). "Further Notes on Images." *Spring 1978*: 152–82.

—— (1979a). *The Dream and the Underworld*. New York: Harper & Row, 1979.

—— (1979b). "Image-Sense." *Spring 1979*: 130–43.

—— (1979c). "The Thought of the Heart." In *Eranos Jahrbuch 48—1979*, pp. 133–82. Frankfurt a/M: Insel Verlag, 1981.

—— (1981a). "Silver and the White Earth (Part Two)." *Spring 1981*: 21–66.

—— (1981b). "Alchemical Blue and the *Unio Mentalis*." *Sulfur* 1 (1981): 33–50.

—— (1982). "*Anima Mundi*: The Return of the Soul to the World." *Spring 1982*: 71–93.

—— and Berry, Patricia (1977). "Archetypal Therapy." Paper: First International Seminar of Archetypal Psychology, University of Dallas, Irving, Texas, 1977.

Hough, Graham (1973). "Poetry and the Anima." *Spring 1973*: 85–96.

Hull, R. F. C. (1971). "Bibliographical Notes on Active Imagination in the Works of C. G. Jung." *Spring 1971*: 115–20.

Hulme, T. E. (1924). *Speculations*. London: Routledge, 1924.

Humbert, Elie (1971). "Active Imagination: Theory and Practice." *Spring 1971*: 101–14.

James, William (1909). *A Pluralistic Universe*. London, 1909.

Jung, C. G. *The Collected Works (CW)*. Translated by R. F. C. Hull. Bollingen Series XX, vols. 1–20, paragraph nos. Princeton: Princeton University Press, 1953 ff.

Jung, Emma (1957). *Animus and Anima*. Spring Publications, 1957.

Kelly, George (1955). *The Psychology of Personal Constructs*. 2 vols. New York: Norton, 1955.

Kugelmann, Robert. *The Windows of Soul: Psychological Physiology of the Human Eye and Primary Glaucoma*. Lewisburg, Pennsylvania: Bucknell University Press, forthcoming.

Kugler, Paul K. (1978). "Image and Sound." *Spring 1978*: 136–51.

——— (1979a). "The Phonetic Imagination." *Spring 1979*: 118–29.

——— (1979b). *The Alchemy of Discourse: An Archetypal Approach to Language*. Dissertation, C. G. Jung Institute, Zürich, 1979 [Lewisburg, Pennsylvania: Bucknell University Press, 1982].

Leveranz, John (1979). "The Sacred Disease." *Dragonflies: Studies in Imaginal Psychology* 1 (1979): 18–38.

Lockhart, Russell A. (1977). "Cancer in Myth and Disease." *Spring 1977*: 1–26.

——— (1978). "Words as Eggs." *Dragonflies: Studies in Imaginal Psychology* 1 (1978): 3–32.

——— (1980). "Psyche in Hiding." *Quadrant* 13 (1980): 76–105.

Lopez-Pedraza, Rafael (1977). *Hermes and His Children*. Spring Publications, 1977.

—— (1982). "Moon Madness—Titanic Love: A Meeting of Pathology and Poetry." In *Images of the Untouched*, edited by J. Stroud and G. Thomas, pp. 11–26. Spring Publications, 1982.

McConeghey, Howard (1981). "Art Education and Archetypal Psychology." *Spring 1981*: 127–35.

Micklem, Niel (1979). "The Intolerable Image: The Mythic Background of Psychosis." *Spring 1979*: 1–18.

Miller, David L. (1972). "Polytheism and Archetypal Theology." *Journal of the American Academy of Religion* 40 (1972): 513–27.

—— (1974). *The New Polytheism*. New York: Harper & Row, 1974 [reissued: with appendix "Psychology: Monotheistic or Polytheistic" (J. Hillman). Spring Publications, 1981].

—— (1976a). "Fairy Tale or Myth." *Spring 1976*: 157–64.

—— (1976b). "Mythopoesis, Psychopoesis, Theopoesis: The Poetries of Meaning." Panarion Conference tape, 1976.

—— (1977). "Imaginings No End." In *Eranos Jahrbuch 46—1977*, pp. 451–500. Leiden: E. J. Brill, 1981.

—— (1981a). *Christs: Meditations on Archetypal Images in Christian Theology*. New York: The Seabury Press, 1981.

—— (1981b). "The Two Sandals of Christ: Descent into History and into Hell." In *Eranos Jahrbuch 50—1981*, pp. 147–221. Frankfurt a/M: Insel Verlag, 1982.

Moore, Tom (1978). "Musical Therapy." *Spring 1978*: 128–35.

—— (1979a). "Artemis and the Puer." In *Puer Papers*, pp. 169–204. Spring Publications, 1979.

—— (1979b). "Images in Asthma: Notes for a Study of Disease." *Dragonflies: Studies in Imaginal Psychology* 1 (1979): 3–14.

—— (1980). "James Hillman: Psychology with Soul." *Religious Studies Review* 6 (1980): 278–84.

—— (1982). *The Planets Within*. Lewisburg, Pennsylvania: Bucknell University Press, 1982.

Newman, K. D. (1980). "Counter-Transference and Consciousness." *Spring 1980*: 117–27.

Ogilvy, James (1977). *Many-Dimensional Man: Decentralizing Self, Society and the Sacred*. New York: Oxford University Press, 1977.

Ritsema, Rudolf (1976). "On the Syntax of the Imaginal." *Spring 1976*: 191–94.

Romanyshyn, Robert (1977). "Remarks on the Metaphorical Basis of Psychological Life." Paper: First International Seminar on Archetypal Psychology, University of Dallas, 1977.

—— (1978–79). "Psychological Language and the Voice of Things" (I and II). *Dragonflies: Studies in Imaginal Psychology* 1 (1978, 1979): 74–90, 73–79.

Sardello, Robert J. (1978a). "Ensouling Language." *Dragonflies: Studies in Imaginal Psychology* 1 (1978): 1–2.

—— (1978b). "An Empirical–Phenomenological Study of Fantasy." *Psychocultural Review* 2 (1978).

—— (1979a). "Imagination and the Transformation of the Perceptual World." Paper: Third American Conference on Fantasy and the Imaging Process, New York, 1979.

—— (1979b). *Educating with Soul*. Pamphlet, Center for Civic Leadership, University of Dallas, 1979.

———— (1980a). "The Mythos of Medicine." In *Medicine and Literature*, edited by K. Rabuzzi. Austin: University of Texas Press, forthcoming.

———— (1980b). "Beauty and Violence: The Play of Imagination in the World." *Dragonflies: Studies in Imaginal Psychology* 2 (1980): 91–104.

———— et al. (1978). *Dragonflies: Studies in Imaginal Psychology* 1 (1978).

Scott, Charles E. (1980). "On Hillman and Calvin." *Soundings* 63 (1980): 61–73.

Severson, Randolph (1978). "Titans Under Glass: A Recipe for the Recovery of Psychological Jargon." *Dragonflies: Studies in Imaginal Psychology* 1 (1978): 64–73.

———— (1979). "Puer's Wounded Wing: Reflections on the Psychology of Skin Disease." In *Puer Papers*, pp. 129–51. Spring Publications, 1979.

Simmer, Stephen (1981). "The Academy of the Dead: On Boredom, Writer's Block, Footnotes and Deadlines." *Spring 1981*: 89–106.

Sipiora, Michael P. (1981). "A Soul's Journey: Camus, Tuberculosis, and Aphrodite." *Spring 1981*: 163–76.

Stein, Murray (1973). "Hephaistos: A Pattern of Introversion." *Spring 1973*: 35–51.

———— (1977). "Hera: Bound and Unbound." *Spring 1977*: 105–19.

Stein, Robert (1974). *Incest and Human Love*. Baltimore: Penguin Books, 1974.

Vico, Giambattista. *Scienza Nuova*. Napoli, 1744 [in translation: *The New Science*. Ithaca: Cornell University Press, 1968].

Vitale, Augusto (1973). "Saturn: The Transformation of the Father." In *Fathers and Mothers: Five Papers on the Archetypal Background of Family Psychology*, edited by Patricia Berry, pp. 5–39. Spring Publications, 1973.

de Voogd, Stephanie (1977). "C. G. Jung: Psychologist of the Future, 'Philosopher' of the Past." *Spring 1977*: 175–82.

Watkins, Mary M. (1976). *Waking Dreams*. New York: Gordon & Breach, 1976.

—— (1981). "Six Approaches to the Image in Art Therapy." *Spring 1981*: 107–25.

Wind, Edgar (1967). *Pagan Mysteries in the Renaissance*. Harmondsworth, England: Peregrine, 1967.

Winquist, Charles (1981). "The Epistemology of Darkness." *Journal of the American Academy of Religion* 49 (1981): 23–34.

Yates, Frances (1966). *The Art of Memory*. London: Routledge, 1966.

Ziegler, A. J. (1980). *Morbismus: Archetypisches Medizin*. Zürich: Raben Reihe, Schweizer Spiegel Verlag, 1980.

Part Three

Complete Checklist of Works
by James Hillman
(through September 1988)

A. Books and Monographs

A60 *Emotion: A Comprehensive Phenomenology of Theories and Their Meanings for Therapy*. London: Routledge & Kegan Paul, and Evanston: Northwestern University Press, 1960.

A64 *Suicide and the Soul*. London: Hodder and Stoughton, and New York: Harper & Row, 1964 [Harper Colophon edition, 1973]. Dallas: Spring Publications, 1976.

A67 *Insearch: Psychology and Religion*. London: Hodder and Stoughton, and New York: Charles Scribner's Sons, 1967. Spring Publications, 1979.

A72 *The Myth of Analysis: Three Essays in Archetypal Psychology*. Evanston: Northwestern University Press, 1972 [Harper Colophon edition, New York: Harper & Row, 1978].

A75a *Loose Ends: Primary Papers in Archetypal Psychology*. New York/Zürich: Spring Publications, 1975.

A75b *Re-Visioning Psychology*. New York: Harper & Row, 1975 [Harper Colophon edition, 1977].

A79 *The Dream and the Underworld*. New York: Harper & Row, 1979.

A83a *Healing Fiction*. Barrytown, N.Y.: Station Hill Press, 1983.

A83b *Archetypal Psychology: A Brief Account.* Dallas: Spring Publications, 1983. Reprinted with Addendum to Checklist 1985 and with a revised Checklist 1988.

A84   *The Thought of the Heart.* Eranos Lectures Series 2. Dallas: Spring Publications, 1984.

A85   *Anima: An Anatomy of a Personified Notion* [with excerpts from the writings of C. G. Jung and original drawings by Mary Vernon]. Dallas: Spring Publications, 1985.

A86   *Egalitarian Typologies versus the Perception of the Unique.* Eranos Lectures Series 4. Dallas: Spring Publications, 1986.

A88   *On Paranoia.* Eranos Lectures Series 8. Dallas: Spring Publications, 1988.

B. Collaborative Volumes

B67   "A Psychological Commentary" to *Kundalini: The Evolutionary Energy in Man,* by Gopi Krishna. New Delhi/Zürich: Ramadhar and Hopman, 1967. London: Stuart and Watkins, and Berkeley: Shambhala, 1970.

B71   "The Feeling Function." In *Lectures on Jung's Typology* [with "The Inferior Function," by Marie-Louise von Franz], pp. 74–150. New York/Zürich: Spring Publications, 1971.

B72   "An Essay on Pan." In *Pan and the Nightmare* [with "Ephialtes: A Pathological–Mythological Treatise on the Nightmare in Classical Antiquity," by W. H. Roscher], pp. 3–65 and p. 156. New York/Zürich: Spring Publications, 1972.

B83   *Inter Views: Conversations between James Hillman and Laura Pozzo on Therapy, Biography, Love, Soul, Dreams, Work, Imagination and the State of the Culture.* New York: Harper & Row, 1983.

B85   *Freud's Own Cookbook* [with Charles Boer]. New York: Harper & Row, 1985.

C. Edited Volumes

C¹   [Associate Editor]. *Envoy: An Irish Review of Literature and Art.* 16 issues. Dublin, 1949–51.

C²   *Students' Association Publications* of the C. G. Jung Institute. 3 pamphlets. Zürich, 1957–58.

C³   *Studies in Jungian Thought.* 11 vols. Evanston: Northwestern University Press, 1967–74; Lewisburg: Bucknell University Press, 1979– .

C⁴   *Spring: An Annual of Archetypal Psychology and Jungian Thought.* 19 vols. New York, Zürich, Irving, Dallas, 1970– . [Starting in 1988, subtitle is *An Annual of Archetype and Culture.*]

C63   *The Logos of the Soul,* by Evangelos Christou. Vienna/Zürich: Dunquin Press, 1963, and Dallas: Spring Publications, 1987.

C79   *Puer Papers.* Dallas: Spring Publications, 1979.

C80   *Facing the Gods.* Dallas: Spring Publications, 1980.

D. Published Essays and Lectures

D62a   "Friends and Enemies." *Harvest* 8 (1962): 1–22.

D62b   "Training and the C. G. Jung Institute, Zürich," "A Note on Multiple Analysis and Emotional Climate in Training Institutes," and "Reply to Discussions." *Journal of Analytical Psychology* 7 (1962): 3–22, 27–28.

D63   "Methodologische Probleme in der Traumforschung." Translated by Hilde Binswanger. In *Traum und Symbol,* edited by C. A. Meier, pp. 91–121. Zürich: Rascher Verlag, 1963. Collected in English without bibliography in A75a.

D64   "Betrayal." Lecture 128, London: Guild of Pastoral Psychology, 1964. Reprinted in *Spring 1965*: 57–76 and in A75a.

D66   "Towards the Archetypal Model for the Masturbation Inhibition." *Journal of Analytical Psychology* 11/1 (1966): 49–62.

Reprinted in *The Reality of the Psyche*, edited by J. Wheelwright [New York: Putnam's, 1968] and in A75a.

D68   "C. G. Jung on Emotion." In *The Nature of Emotion*, edited by M. B. Arnold, pp. 125-34. Harmondsworth: Penguin Books, 1968.

D70a   "C. G. Jung's Contribution to Feelings and Emotions: Synopsis and Implications." In *Feelings and Emotions*, edited by M. B. Arnold, pp. 125-35. New York: Academic Press, 1970.

D70b   "An Imaginal Ego." In *Inscape 2*, pp. 2-8. London: British Association of Art Therapists, 1970.

D70c   "On Senex Consciousness." *Spring 1970*: 146-65.

D70d   "Why 'Archetypal' Psychology?" *Spring 1970*: 212-19. Reprinted with postscript in A75a.

D71a   "Psychology: Monotheistic or Polytheistic?" *Spring 1971*: 193-208, 230-32. Expanded in Appendix to *The New Polytheism*, by David Miller, pp. 109-42 [Dallas: Spring Publications, 1981].

D71b   "On the Psychology of Parapsychology." In *A Century of Psychical Research*, edited by A. Angoff and B. Shapin, pp. 176-87. New York: Parapsychology Foundation, 1971. Reprinted in A75a.

D72a   "Dionysos in Jung's Writings." *Spring 1972*: 191-205. Reprinted in C80, pp. 151-64.

D72b   "Three Ways of Failure and Analysis." *Journal of Analytical Psychology* 17/1 (1972): 1-6. Reprinted in *Success and Failure in Analysis*, edited by G. Adler [New York: Putnam's, 1974] and in A75a.

D72c   "Schism: As Differing Visions." Lecture 162, London: Guild of Pastoral Psychology, 1972. Reprinted in A75a.

D73a   "Anima." *Spring 1973*: 97-132. Expanded in A85.

D73b   "Pathologizing (or Falling Apart)." *Art International/Lugano Review* 17/6 (1973). Revised in A75b.

D73c   "The Great Mother, Her Son, Her Hero, and the Puer." In *Fathers and Mothers: Five Papers on the Archetypal Background of Family Psychology*, edited by P. Berry, pp. 75-127. New York/ Zürich: Spring Publications, 1973.

D73d   "Plotino, Ficino e Vico precursori della psicologia degli archetipi."

Rivista di psicologia analitica 4 (1973): 322–40. Reprinted in Italian and English in *Enciclopedia '74*: 55–80. Collected (in English) in A75a.

D74a   "'Anima' (II)." *Spring 1974*: 113–46. Expanded in A85.

D74b   "A Note on Story." *Children's Literature* 3 (1974): 9–11. Reprinted in *Parabola* 4 (1979): 43–45. Collected in A75a.

D74c   "Archetypal Theory: C. G. Jung." In *Operational Theories of Personality*, edited by A. Burton, pp. 65–98. New York: Brunner/Mazel, 1974. Abridged in A75a.

D74d   "*Pothos*: The Nostalgia of the Puer Eternus." Lecture first delivered in French, May 1974, in Chambéry. Collected (in English) in A75a.

D75a   "The Fiction of Case History: A Round." In *Religion as Story*, edited by J. B. Wiggins, pp. 123–73. New York: Harper & Row, 1975. Revised in A83a.

D75b   "The 'Negative' Senex and a Renaissance Solution." *Spring 1975*: 77–109.

D76a   "Peaks and Vales: The Soul / Spirit Distinction as Basis for the Differences between Psychotherapy and Spiritual Discipline." In *On the Way to Self-Knowledge*, edited by J. Needleman and D. Lewis, pp. 114–47. New York: Knopf, 1976. Collected in C79, pp. 54–74.

D76b   "Some Early Background to Jung's Ideas: Notes on C. G. *Jung's Medium* by Stefanie Zumstein-Preiswerk." *Spring 1976*: 123–36.

D77a   "An Inquiry into Image." *Spring 1977*: 62–88.

D77b   "The Pandaemonium of Images: C. G. Jung's Contribution to *Know Thyself*." *New Lugano Review/Art International* 3 (1977): 35–45. Revised in A83a. First publication in German, E75.

D78a   *City and Soul*. Irving: Center for Civic Leadership, University of Dallas, 1978. Reprinted in *Vision Magazine*, October 1978, 27–29. Reprinted in *Dromenon* 4 (1982): 57–59, in *Tarrytown Letter* 25 [The Tarrytown Group] (1983), and in *Urban Resources* 1/4 (1984): 36 and 42.

D78b   "Further Notes on Images." *Spring 1978*: 152–82.

D78c   "Therapeutic Value of Alchemical Language." *Dragonflies: Studies* in *Imaginal Psychology* 1/1 (1978): 33–42. Reprinted in *Methods of Treatment in Analytical Psychology*, edited by I. F. Baker, pp. 118–26 [Fellbach: Verlag Adolf Bonz, 1980].

D79a   "Image-Sense." *Spring 1979*: 130–43.

D79b   "Notes on Opportunism." In C79, pp. 152–65.

D79c   "Puer's Wound and Ulysses' Scar." In C79, pp. 100–28. Reprinted in *Dromenon* 3 (1981): 12–27.

D79d   *Psychological Fantasies in Transportation Problems*. Irving: Center for Civic Leadership, University of Dallas, 1979.

D80a   "La Mesure des événements: la proposition 117 de Proclus dans la perspective d'une psychologie archétypique." In *Science et Conscience*, edited by M. Cazenave, pp. 283–99. Paris: Stock, 1980.

D80b   "Take a Walk." *D Magazine*, September 1980, 69–78. Abridgment of "Walking." In *The City as Dwelling*, pp. 1–7. Irving: Center for Civic Leadership, University of Dallas, 1980. Reprinted as "Paradise in Walking," *Resurgence* 129 (1988): 4–7.

D80c   "Silver and the White Earth." *Spring 1980*: 21–48.

D81a   "Alchemical Blue and the *Unio Mentalis*." *Sulfur: A Literary Tri-Quarterly of the Whole Art* 1 (1981): 33–50.

D81b   "Salt: A Chapter in Alchemical Psychology." In *Images of the Untouched*, edited by J. Stroud and G. Thomas, pp. 111–37. Dallas: Spring Publications, 1981.

D81c   "Silver and the White Earth (Part Two)." *Spring 1981*: 21–66.

D81d   "Psicologia Archetipico." In *Enciclopedia del Novecento*, vol. 5, pp. 813–27. Rome: Istituto dell'Enciclopedia Italiana, 1981. Revised in English as A83b.

D82a   *"Anima Mundi*: The Return of the Soul to the World." *Spring 1982*: 71–93.

D82b   "De la certitude mythique." *Cadmos* 5/17–18 (1982): 29–51.

D83   "The Bad Mother: An Archetypal Approach." *Spring 1983*: 165–81.

D84   "Mars, Arms, Rams, Wars: On the Love of War." In *Nuclear Strategy and the Code of the Warrior: Faces of Mars and Shiva in the Crisis of Human Survival*, edited by R. Grossinger and L. Hough, pp. 247-67. Berkeley: North Atlantic Books, 1984. Reprinted as "Wars, Arms, Rams, Mars: On the Love of War," in *Facing Apocalypse*, ed. V. Andrews, R. Bosnak, K. W. Goodwin, pp. 118-36 [Dallas: Spring Publications, 1987].

D85a   "Extending the Family: From Entrapment to Embrace." *The Texas Humanist* 7/4 (1985): 6-11. Reprinted in abbreviated form as "Family: From Entrapment to Embrace," *Utne Reader* 27 (1988): 62-65.

D85b   "Natural Beauty without Nature." *Spring 1985*: 50-55. An expanded version of a talk delivered at the symposium "Present Tense, Future Perfect?" and collected in the report, edited by P. A. Y. Gunter and B. Higgins (Dallas: LandMark Program, 1984), pp. 65-69.

D85c   "The Autonomous Psyche" [with Paul Kugler]. *Spring 1985*: 141-61.

D86a   "Bachelard's Lautréamont, or Psychoanalysis without a Patient." Afterword essay in Gaston Bachelard, *Lautréamont*, translated by Robert S. Dupree, pp. 103-23. Dallas: The Dallas Institute Publications, 1986.

D86b   "Notes on White Supremacy: Essaying an Archetypal Account of Historical Events." *Spring 1986*: 29-58.

D87   "A Psychology of Transgression Drawn from an Incest Dream: Imagining the Case." *Spring 1987*: 66-76.

D88a   "Sex Talk: Imagining a New Male Sexuality." *Utne Reader* 29 (1988): 76.

D88b   "Power and Gemeinschaftsgefühl." *Individual Psychology: The Journal of Adlerian Theory, Research and Practice* 44/1 (1988): 3-12.

D88c   "Going Bugs." *Spring 1988*: 40-72.

D88d   "Jung's Daimonic Inheritance." *Sphinx* 1 (1988): 9-19. First published as "Il demoniaco come eredità di Jung," in *Presenza ed eredità culturale di C. G. Jung*, edited by L. Zoja, pp. 93-102. Milan: Cortina, 1987.

D88e   "The Right to Remain Silent." *Journal of Humanistic Education and Development* 26/4 (1988): 141-53. First published as "Del dir-

itto a non parlare," translated by Beatrice Rebecchi, *l'immaginale* 9 (1987): 19–33.

E. Contributions to the Eranos Jahrbuch

E66   "On Psychological Creativity." In *Eranos Jahrbuch 35—1966*,
pp. 349–410. Zürich: Rhein, 1967. Reprinted in *Art International* 13/7 (1969). Revised in A72.

E67   "Senex and Puer: An Aspect of the Historical and Psychological
Present." In *Eranos Jahrbuch 36—1967*, pp. 301-60. Zürich:
Rhein, 1969. Reprinted in *Art International* 15/1 (1971). Col-
lected in C79, pp. 3–53.

E68   "The Language of Psychology and the Speech of the Soul." In
Eranos Jahrbuch 37—1968, pp. 299–356. Zürich: Rhein, 1970.
Also in *Art International* 14/1 (1970). Revised in A72.

E69   "First Adam, then Eve: Fantasies of Female Inferiority in Chang-
ing Consciousness." In *Eranos Jahrbuch 38—1969*, pp. 349–412.
Zürich: Rhein, 1972. Also in *Art International* 14/7 (1970).
Revised in A72.

E71   "Abandoning the Child." In *Eranos Jahrbuch 40—1971*,
pp. 358–406. Leiden: E. J. Brill, 1973. Revised in A75a.

E73   "The Dream and the Underworld." In *Eranos Jahrbuch
42—1973*, pp. 91–136. Leiden: E. J. Brill, 1977. Expanded in
A79.

E74   "On the Necessity of Abnormal Psychology." In *Eranos Jahrbuch
43—1974*, pp. 91–135. Leiden: E. J. Brill, 1977. Reprinted in
C80, pp. 1–38.

E75   "Pandämonium der Bilder: C. G. Jungs Beitrag zum 'Erkenne dich
Selbst.'" Translated by Philipp Wolff. In *Eranos Jahrbuch
44—1975*, pp. 415-52. Leiden: E. J. Brill, 1977. In English: included in A83a; D77b.

E76   "Egalitarian Typologies *versus* the Perception of the Unique."
In *Eranos Jahrbuch 45—1976*, pp. 221–80. Leiden: E. J. Brill,
1980. Reprinted as A86.

E77   "Psychotherapy's Inferiority Complex." In *Eranos Jahrbuch 46—1977*, pp. 121-74. Frankfurt a/M: Insel Verlag, 1981. Revised in A83a.

E79   "The Thought of the Heart." In *Eranos Jahrbuch 48—1979*, pp. 133-82. Frankfurt a/M: Insel Verlag, 1981. Reprinted as A84.

E81   "The Imagination of Air and the Collapse of Alchemy." In *Eranos Jahrbuch 50—1981*, pp. 273-333. Frankfurt a/M: Insel Verlag, 1982.

E82   "The Animal Kingdom in the Human Dream." In *Eranos Jahrbuch 51—1982*, pp. 279-334. Frankfurt a/M: Insel Verlag, 1983.

E85   "On Paranoia." In *Eranos Jahrbuch 54—1985*, pp. 269-324. Frankfurt a/M: Insel Verlag, 1987. Reprinted as A88.

E87   "Oedipus Revisited." In *Eranos Jahrbuch 56—1987*. Frankfurt a/M: Insel Verlag, forthcoming.

F. Prefaces, Interviews, Translations, and Occasional Writings

F57   "Editor's Preface" to *The Transcendent Function*, by C. G. Jung, translated by A. R. Pope [privately printed]. Zürich: Students' Association of the C. G. Jung Institute, 1957.

F63a   "Foreword" [with A. K. Donoghue] to *The Cocaine Papers*, by Sigmund Freud, pp. iii–viii. Vienna/Zürich: Dunquin Press and Spring Publications, 1963.

F63b   "Freunde und Feinde" [with Adolf Guggenbühl-Craig]. *Schweizer Spiegel* 38 (1963): 21-26.

F63c   "Editor's Introduction" to *The Logos of the Soul*, by Evangelos Christou, pp. i–iv. Vienna/Zürich: Dunquin Press, 1963 (re-issued Dallas: Spring Publications, 1987).

F67a   "Preface to the American Edition" of *Evil*. Evanston: Northwestern University Press, 1967.

F67b   "Preface" to *Satan in the Old Testament*, by Rivkah Schärf Kluger. Evanston: Northwestern University Press, 1967.

F67c   "Preface to the American Edition" in *Ancient Incubation and Modern Psychotherapy*, by C. A. Meier. Evanston: Northwestern University Press, 1967.

F67d   "De psychologie van het kwaad." *Elseviers Weekblad* 23 (1967): 33–34.

F68a   "Editor's Preface to the American Edition" of *Timeless Documents of the Soul*, by S. Hurwitz, M.-L. von Franz and H. Jacobsohn. Evanston: Northwestern University Press, 1968.

F68b   "A Psychologist Talks about . . ." [Interview with James Hillman, by Kenneth L. Wilson]. *Christian Herald* 91 (1968): 22–28, 54–58.

F69   "Ein Kampf auf Leben und Tod? Bermerkungen zum Aufstand der Jugend" [with Adolf Guggenbühl-Craig]. *Schweizer Spiegel* 44 (1969): 16–22.

F70a   "An Introductory Note: C. G. Carus–C. G. Jung" in *Psyche (Part One)*, by Carl Gustav Carus. New York/Zürich: Spring Publications, 1970.

F70b   "Preface to the American Edition" of *Conscience*. Evanston: Northwestern University Press, 1970.

F70c   Translation, from German, of "Must Analysis Fail through Its Destructive Aspect?" by Adolf Guggenbühl-Craig. *Spring 1970*: 133–45.

F71   "Avant Propos" to the *Catalogue of Cecil Collins: Recent Paintings*. London: Arthur Tooth and Sons, 1971.

F76   "Publisher's Prefatory Note" to *The Visions Seminars*, by C. G. Jung. Zürich/New York: Spring Publications, 1976.

F77a   "Letter" [on Jung's style compared with T. S. Eliot's]. *Journal of Analytical Psychology* 22 (1977): 59.

F77b   "Publisher's Preface" to *Hermes and His Children*, by Rafael Lopez-Pedraza. Zürich: Spring Publications, 1977.

F79   "Letter from the Editor for a Tenth Anniversary." *Spring 1979*: i–ii.

F80a   "The Children, the Children! An Editorial." *Children's Literature* 8 (1980): 3–6.

F80b   "Editor's Preface" to *Facing the Gods* (C80), p. iv.

F80c   "Letter to the Editor." *D Magazine*, December 1980, 8.

F80d   "Compagnon d'Eranos, communion invisible." In *La Galaxie de l'Imaginaire, dérivé autour de l'oeuvre de Gilbert Durand*, edited by M. Maffesoli, pp. 217–20. Paris: Berg International, 1980.

F81a   "Entertaining Ideas." *The Institute Newsletter* 1/1 [The Dallas Institute of Humanities and Culture] (1981): 5–7. Reprinted in *Stirrings of Culture*, edited by R. Sardello and G. Thomas, pp. 3–5 [Dallas: The Dallas Institute Publications, 1986].

F81b   "Letter to Tom Moore." *Corona* 2 (1981): 115–20.

F81c   "Vorwort zur 2. Auflage in deutscher Sprache" to *Die Suche nach Innen*, pp. i–ii. Zürich: Daimon Verlag, 1981. See GeA67.

F82a   "A Contribution to Soul and Money." In *Soul and Money*, by Russell A. Lockhart, James Hillman et al., pp. 31–43. Dallas: Spring Publications, 1982. Reprinted in *Money, Food, Drink and Fashion and Analytic Training: Depth Dimensions of Physical Existence* (The Proceedings of the Eighth International Congress For Analytical Psychology), edited by J. Beebe, pp. 52–59 [Fellbach: Verlag Adolf Bonz, 1983].

F82b   "On Culture and Chronic Disorder." *The Institute Newsletter* 1/2 [The Dallas Institute of Humanities and Culture] (1982): 12–17. Reprinted in *Stirrings of Culture*, pp. 15–21.

F82c   "City Limits." In *Imagining Dallas*, pp. 55–63. Dallas: The Dallas Institute of Humanities and Culture, 1982.

F83a   "Interiors in the Design of the City: The Ceiling." *The Institute Newsletter* 2/1 [The Dallas Institute of Humanities and Culture] (1983): 11–18. Reprinted as "Interior and Design of the City: Ceilings," in *Stirrings of Culture*, pp. 78–84. Excerpt published as "One Man's Ceiling Is Another Man's Horror," *Utne Reader* 8 (1985): 104.

F83b   "Let the Creatures Be" [with Tom Moore]. *Parabola* 8/2 (1983): 49–53.

F83c   "Jungian Psychology and Oriental Thought" [with Toshihiko Izutsu and Hayao Kawai]. Translated into Japanese by Mrs.

Izutsu. *Shiso* 6/708 (1983): 1–35.

F83d   "Buffalo's Inner City: A Conversation between Paul Kugler and James Hillman." *Buffalo Arts Review* 1/1 (1983): 1 and 6–7.

F83e   "Letter to the Editor" [with Paul Kugler]. *Buffalo Arts Review* 1/2 (1983).

F83f   Translation, from German, of "Jottings on the Jung Film *Matter of Heart*," by Adolf Guggenbühl-Craig. *Spring 1983*: 199–202.

F84a   "Talking as Walking." *The Institute Newsletter* [The Dallas Institute of Humanities and Culture] (Fall 1984): 10–12. Reprinted in *Stirrings of Culture*, pp. 12–14.

F84b   "Souls Take Pleasure in Moisture." *The Institute Newsletter* [The Dallas Institute of Humanities and Culture] (Fall 1984): 35–38. Reprinted in *Stirrings of Culture*, pp. 203–05.

F84c   "The Spirit of the City." *Buffalo Arts Review* 2/1 (1984): 3 and 5.

F84d   "Une psychologie archétypale, entretien James Hillman/Michel Cazenave." In *Carl G. Jung*, Cahier de l'Herne, no. 46, pp. 491–99. Paris: l'Herne, 1984.

F85a   "The Wildman in the Cage." *Voices: Journal of the American Academy of Psychotherapists* (1985): 30–34. Reprinted as "The Wildman in the Cage: Comment," in *New Men, New Minds: Breaking Male Tradition*, edited by F. Abbott, pp. 182–86 [Freedom, CA.: Crossing Press, 1987].

F85b   "In Memoriam Robert Grinnell," edited by C. Goodrich [privately printed]. Santa Barbara, 1985.

F85c   "James Hillman on Animals: A Correspondence with John Stockwell." *Between the Species* 1/2 (1985): 4–8. Excerpted in *Utne Reader* 19 (1987): 66–67.

F85d   "Prefazione" to *Trame perdute*, by James Hillman, pp. xi–xiii. Milan: Cortina, 1985. See *It85*.

F86a   "Selling out to Developers" [Letter to the Editor]. *Putnam Observer Patriot*, 9 March 1986, 9.

F86b   "A Dialogue with James Hillman" [with Shaun McNiff]. *Art Therapy* 3/3 (1986): 99–110.

F86c   "Part One of a Discussion on Psychology and Poetry" [with

Clayton Eshleman]. *Sulfur: A Literary Tri-Quarterly of the Whole Art* 6/1 (1986): 56–74.

F86d "Soul and Spirit." In *Carl Jung and Soul Psychology*, edited by E. M. Stern, pp. 29–35. New York: Haworth Press, 1986. Also in *Voices: The Art and Science of Psychotherapy* 21/3 & 4 (1986): 29–35. Excerpts from A64, pp. 43–47, and A75b, pp. 67–70.

F87a "Conversation with James Hillman." In *The Search for Omm Sety*, by Jonathan Cott, pp. 221–25. New York: Doubleday, 1987.

F87b "Bureaucratic Buck-Passing." *Putnam Observer Patriot*, 5 February 1987, 5.

F87c "Behind the Iron Grillwork" [for Clayton Eshleman]. *Temblor* 6 (1987): 100.

F88a "James Hillman on Soul and Spirit: An Interview with Barbara Dunn." *The Common Boundary* 6/4 (1988): 5–11.

F88b "Prefazione" to *Saggi sul puer*, by James Hillman, pp. xi–xiii. Milan: Cortina, 1988. See *It*88.

F89 "Conversation avec James Hillman" [Interview with James Hillman, by Ginette Paris]. *Guide Ressources* (1989): forthcoming.

G. Unpublished Writings

G65 "The Courage to Risk Failure." Graduation address delivered June 1965 at the American International School of Zürich.

G67a "Life and Death in Analysis." Paper delivered at an international conference on suicide, October 1967, San Francisco State University.

G67b "Symbols of Dying." Paper delivered at an international conference on suicide, October 1967, San Francisco State University.

G70 "The Problem of Fantasies and the Fantasy of Problems." Lecture held November 1969 in Brighton. Mimeographed. London: Centre for Spiritual and Psychological Studies, 1970.

G71 "Guidelines for the Future." Lecture held 24 April 1971 in

Malvern, England. Mimeographed. London: Centre for Spiritual and Psychological Studies.

G77   "Archetypal Therapy" [with Patricia Berry]. Paper presented January 1977 at the "First International Seminar of Archetypal Psychology," University of Dallas, Irving, Texas, 1977.

G79a   "Goals for Dallas: Dallas for Goals." Lecture delivered June 1979 to department heads and subheads of the City of Dallas.

G79b   "On Graduate Despond." Graduate Dean's opening semester address, September 1979, to the Institute of Philosophic Studies, University of Dallas, Irving, Texas.

G80   "Respect for Air." Contribution to a panel on inspection and maintenance of automobile exhaust emissions, September 1980, Dallas City Hall.

G81   "Imagination is Bull." Lecture delivered March 1981 at The Dallas Institute of Humanities and Culture.

G83a   "Back to the Beyond: On Cosmology" [together with "Responses" to Edward Casey, David Griffin and Murray Stein]. Opening address to the conference "Whitehead, Jung and Hillman," February 1983, at the Center for Process Studies, Claremont, California. Included in *Process and Archetype: Self and Divine in Jung, Hillman and Whitehead*, edited by D. Griffin. Evanston: Northwestern University Press, forthcoming.

G83b   "On Dreaming of Pigs: A Jungian View of Interpretation." Lecture delivered November 1983 under the auspices of the Department of English, Yale University, New Haven, Connecticut.

G86a   "Cosmology for Soul: From Universe to Cosmos" [with "Panel Discussions"]. Lecture delivered at Tenri International Symposium "Cosmos–Life–Religion: Beyond Humanism," December 1986, Tenri University, Nara, Japan. Proceedings forthcoming from Tenri University Press.

G86b   "Introduction" and "Conversation" in panel on "Jung and the Post-Modern Condition." "C. G. Jung and the Humanities" conference, November 1986, Hofstra University, Hempstead, New York. Proceedings forthcoming from Princeton University Press.

G86c   "Conversation" and "Replies" in panel on "Creativity." "C. G. Jung and the Humanities" conference.

G86d   "The Elephant in *The Garden of Eden*." Paper delivered in honor of the Ernest Hemingway Year, October 1986, Boise State University, Boise, Idaho.

G87   "The Open City." Keynote address at "The Soul of Pittsburgh" conference, May 1987, Urban Redevelopment Authority and C. G. Jung Center, Pittsburgh.

G88a   "Show-Business Ethics." Paper delivered at the annual conference "What Makes a City," May 1988, The Dallas Institute of Humanities and Culture.

G88b   "The Art of the Soul." Keynote talk at the symposium "Embodying the Spiritual in the Art of the Future," September 1988, San Francisco Art Institute.

Translations of A–G

Nota bene: The first two letters of the codes in this section refer to the language into which the work has been translated. The remaining characters identify the work in its original form (from sections A through G). If the translation is a collection of various works, the code will be only the language and date of publication. These collections are found at the ends of language sections.

Danish

DaA64   *Selvmord og sjaelelig forvandling.* Translated by Dita Mendel [Afterword by Eigil Nyborg]. Copenhagen: Rhodos, 1978.

Dutch

DuA67   *Zelfonderzoek.* Translated by Frits Lancel. Rotterdam: Lemniscaat, 1969.

DuA75a   *Verraad en verlangen: beelden uit de archetypische psychologie* [only

Parts 1–5]. Translated by Els Pikaar. Rotterdam: Lemniscaat, 1984.

French

FrE67   "Kronos—Senex et Puer." Translated by Monique Salzmann. *Cahiers de psychologie jungienne* 18 (1978): 36–55.

FrA72   *Le mythe de la psychanalyse.* Translated by Philippe Mikriammos. Paris: Imago, 1977.

FrB72   *Pan et le cauchemar.* Translated by Th. Auzas, Marie-Jeanne Benmussa and Monique Salzmann. Paris: Imago, 1979.

FrD73a/ "Anima." Translated by Viviane Thibaudier. In *Anima et Animus*
 D74a   [with Emma Jung], pp. 109–221. Paris: Seghers, 1981.

FrF77b   "Préface" to *Hermes et ses enfants dans la psychothérapie,* by Rafael Lopez-Pedraza. Translated by Marie-Jeanne Benmussa and Th. Auzas. Paris: Imago, 1980.

FrF82b   "La culture et la chronicité du désordre." Translated by Michèle-Isis Brouillet. *La petite revue de philosophie* 9/2 (1988): 11–25.

FrB85   *La cuisine de Freud* [with Charles Boer]. Translated by Anne Ledoux-Mabille and Micheline Drain. Paris: Payot, 1985.

Fr82   *Le polythéisme de l'âme.* Translated by Thomas Johnson. Paris: Mercure de France–Le Mail, 1982. Includes C80, pp. 1–38, D76a, and the expanded version of D71a published in *The New Polytheism.*

See also D80a, D82b, F80d, F84d, F89.

German

GeA64   *Selbstmord und seelische Wandlung.* Translated by Hilde Binswanger [Foreword by Adolf Guggenbühl-Craig]. Zürich: Rascher Verlag, 1966. Zürich: Schweizer Spiegel Verlag, 1979.

GeD64   "Verrat." Translated by Wolfgang Giegerich and Ruth Horine. *Analytische Psychologie* 10 (1979): 81–102.

GeA67   *Die Begegnung mit sich Selbst.* Translated by Marianne von Eckardt-Jaffé. Stuttgart: Klett Verlag, 1969. 2d edition, with new foreword, under the title *Die Suche nach Innen: Psychologie und Religion*. Zürich: Daimon Verlag, 1981.

GeD70c "Uber das Senex-Bewußtsein." Translated by Gisela Henney. *Gorgo* 3 (1980): 23–42.

GeB71 "Das Gefühl und die Fühlfunktion." In *Zur Typologie C. G. Jungs* [with Marie-Louise von Franz], pp. 105–214. Fellbach: Verlag Adolf Bonz, 1980.

GeD71a "Die Psychologie: monotheistisch oder polytheistisch?" Translated by Gudula Herrmann. *Gorgo* 1 (1979): 1–21.

GeB72 *Pan und die natürliche Angst—über Notwendigkeit der Alpträume für die Seele*. Translated by Trude Fein. Zürich: Raben Reihe, Schweizer Spiegel Verlag, 1981.

GeD73a "Anima." Translated by Hildegard Thevs. *Gorgo* 5 (1981): 45–81.

GeD74a "Anima II." Translated by Gert Quenzer. *Gorgo* 6 (1981): 56–89.

GeA79 *Am Anfang war das Bild: Unsere Traume—Brucke der Seele zu den Mythen*. Translated by Doris Engelke. Munich: Kösel, 1983.

GeF82a "Seele und Geld." Translated by Wolfgang Giegerich. *Gorgo* 4 (1980): 31–40.

GeA83a *Die Heilung erfinden: Eine psychotherapeutische Poetik*. Translated by Käthi Staufer-Zahner. Zürich: Raben Reihe, Schweizer Spiegel Verlag, 1986. An excerpt from Part III was published as "Was will die Seele?" *Analytische Psychologie* 17 (1986): 160–85.

GeB85 *Sigmund Freud: Mein Kochbuch* [with Charles Boer]. Translated by Doris Engelke. Frankfurt a/M: Eichborn Verlag, 1986.

GeD85c "Die autonome Psyche" [with Paul Kugler]. Translated by Wolfgang Giegerich. *Gorgo* 10 (1986): 3–23.

GeD87a "Eine Psychologie der Überschreitung: gewonnen aus einem Inzesttraum." *Gorgo* 13 (1987): 27–39.

See also D63, E75, F63b, F69, F81c.

Italian

ItF63c "Editor's Preface" to *Il Logos dell' Anima*, by Evangelos Christou. Translated by Emilio di Domenici. Rome: Città Nuova, 1987.

ItA64   *Il suicidio e l'anima.* Translated by Aldo Giuliani. Rome: Astrolabio, 1972.

ItD64   "Il Tradimento." *Rivista di psicologia analitica* 2 (1971): 177–98.

ItD66   "Modello archetipico di inibizione alla masturbazione." In *Problemi di psicologia analitica: una antologia post-junghiana,* edited by L. Zoja, pp. 80–98. Naples: Liguori, 1983.

ItA67   "Vita interiore. L'inconscio come esperienza." *Rivista di psicologia analitica* 4 (1973): 67–98. See Chapter One of A67.

ItB67   "Commento psicologico." In *Kundalini,* by Gopi Krishna, translated by Paolo Colombo. Rome: Astrolabio, 1971.

ItE67   *Senex et Puer e il tradimento.* Translated by Matelda Giuliani Talarico. Padua/Venice: Marsilio, 1973. See also ItD64.

ItE68   "Linguaggio della psicologia e linguaggio dell'anima." *Rivista di psicologia analitica* 3 (1972): 308–74.

ItD70d   "Psicologia Archetipica." Translated by Paola Donfrancesco and Robert Tamarri. *l'immaginale* 8 (1987): 25–39.

ItD71a   "Psicologia: Monoteistica o Politeistica." In *Il Nuovo Politeismo* [with David Miller], pp. 115–54. Milan: Comunità, 1983.

ItA72   *Il mito dell'analisi.* Translated by Aldo Giuliani. Milan: Adelphi, 1979.

ItB72   *Saggio su Pan.* Translated by Aldo Giuliani. Milan: Adelphi, 1977.

ItD72b   "Analisi e fallimento." *Rivista di psicologia analitica* 3 (1972): 211–19.

ItD73a   "Anima." *Rivista di psicologia analitica* 21 (1980).

ItD74c   "C. G. Jung e la teoria archetipica." In *Problemi di psicologia analitica, op. cit. sup.,* pp. 50–79.

ItD74d   "Pothos, la nostalgia del puer aeternus." Translated by Francesco and Paola Donfrancesco. *Prassi e Teoria* 4 (1980): 123–36.

ItA75b   *Re-visione della psicologia.* Translated by Aldo Giuliani. Milan: Adelphi, 1983.

ItD76b   "Un primo sfondo al pensiero Jung." Translated by Franca Cassuto. *l'immaginale* 4 (1985): 21–33.

ItD77a   "Richerche sull'immagine." Translated by Ada Bianchi Maffei. *Rivista di psicologia analitica* 20 (1979): 31–63.

ItD77b   "Il pandemonio delle immagini. Il contributo di Jung al 'conosci te stesso.'" Translated by Paola Donfrancesco. *Testimonianze* 23 (1980): 61–90. See E75.

ItD78c   "Il valore terapeutico del linguaggio alchemico." *Rivista di psicologia analitica* 17 (1978): 143–61.

ItA79   *Il Sogno e il mondo infero.* Translated by Paola Donfrancesco. Milan: Comunità, 1984.

ItD81a   "Blu alchemico e unio mentalis." Translated by Milka Ventura and Veronica Park. *l'immaginale* 7 (1986): 33–46.

ItD81b   "Il Sale: un capitolo di psicologia alchimistica." Translated by Sergio Rinaldelli. *Hellas: rivista di letteratura sul mito* 8/9 (1985): 67–86. Published also as "Sale: un capitolo della psicologia alchemica" in *L'Intatta*, edited by J. Stroud and G. Thomas, pp. 132–64. Translated by Marta Cohen Hemsi. Como: Redazionale, 1987.

ItD82a   "Anima Mundi, il ritorno dell'anima al mondo." Translated by Paola Donfrancesco. *Testimonianze* 24 (1981): 123–40. Reprinted in *l'immaginale* 5 (1985): 5–25.

ItD82b   "Della certezza mitica." *l'immaginale* 6 (1986): 63–80.

ItA83a   *Le storie che curano.* Translated by Milka Ventura and Paola Donfrancesco. Milan: Cortina, 1984.

ItB83   *Intervista su amore, anima e psiche* [with Marina Beer]. Bari: Laterza, 1983. Expanded in B83. Chapter 9 of B83 is published as "Sul mio scrivere," translated by Maria Rosaria Buri, *l'immaginale* 2 (1984): 5–17.

ItB85   *La cucina del dottor Freud* [with Charles Boer]. Translated by Vittorio Serra Boccara. Milan: Cortina, 1986.

ItD86b   "Sulla supremazia del bianco." Translated by Beatrice Rebecchi Cecconi. *l'immaginale* 10 (1988): 5–35.

It85   *Trame perdute.* Translated by several hands. Milan: Cortina, 1985. Selections from A75a and also containing B71, D70b, D75b, D83a, F82b.

It88   *Saggi sul puer.* Translated by Paola Donfrancesco, Milka Ventura, and Silvia Lagorio. Milan: Cortina, 1988. Includes D73c, D74d, D76a, D79b, D79c.

See also D73d, D81d, D88d, D88e, F85d, F88b.

Japanese

JaA64   *Jisatsu to Tamashii*. Translated by Kazuhiko Higuchi. Tokyo: So-gen Sha, 1982.

JaA67   [*Insearch*]. Tokyo: Sogen Sha, forthcoming.

JaA79   [*The Dream and the Underworld*]. Tokyo: Sogen Sha, forthcoming.

JaA83b   [*Archetypal Psychology*]. Tokyo: Sogen Sha, forthcoming.

JaD83a   "Bad Mother, Good Child," translated by Tsuneko Matsuo. In *Parents-Child Bonding: Interdisciplinary Approaches*, edited by Kawai, Kobayashi, and Nakane, pp. 258–76. Osaka: Sogen Sha, 1984.

See also F83c.

Portuguese

PoA64   [*Suicide and the Soul*]. São Paulo: Arte Ciencia, forthcoming.

PoA67   *Una Busca interior em psicologia e religião*. Translated by Aracéli Martins and José Joaquim Sobral. São Paulo: Ed. Paulinas, 1985.

PoB67   "Comentários Psicológicos" to *Kundalini*, by Gopi Krishna. Trans-lated by Ernesto Bono. Rio de Janeiro: Edit. Record., n.d.

PoB71   [The Feeling Function]. São Paulo: Editora Cultrix, forthcoming.

PoA72   *O Mito da Análise*. Translated by Norma Telles. Rio de Janeiro: Paz e Terra, 1984.

PoD73c   "A Grande Mae, seu Filho, seu Heroi, e O Puer." Translated by Pedro Penteado Kujawski. In *Pais e Maes*, pp. 97–153. São Paulo: Símbolo, 1979.

PoA75a   *Estudos de Psicológia Arquetípica*. Translated by Pedro Ratis e Silva. Rio de Janeiro: Achiamé, 1981.

PoD76a   "Picos e Vales." Translated by Adelaide Petters Lessa. In *No Caminho do Autoconhecimento*, pp. 91–118. São Paulo: Livraria Pioneira, 1982.

PoB83   [*Inter Views*]. São Paulo: Arte Ciencia, forthcoming.

PoB85   O *Livro de Cozhina do Dr. Freud* [with Charles Boer]. Translated by Silvio Cancellotti. São Paulo: Paz e Terra, 1986.

Spanish

SpF77b   "Prefacio a la Edición en Lengua Hispánica" to *Hermes y sus Hijos*, by Rafael Lopez-Pedraza. Translated by Carlos Valbuena. Caracas: Editorial Ateneo, 1980.

Swedish

SwA64   *Sjalvmordet och själen*. Translated by Gudrun Ullman. Stockholm: Rabén och Sjögren, 1967.

Also by James Hillman from Spring Publications

Anima: An Anatomy of a Personified Notion

Anima and Eros, Anima and Feeling, Anima and the Feminine, Anima and Psyche, Mediatrix of the Unknown, Integration of the Anima, etc.—ten succinct chapters, accompanied by relevant quotations from Jung (on left-hand pages facing Hillman's essay), which clarify the moods, persons, and definitions of the most subtle and elusive aspect of psychology and of life. Illustrated. (188 pp.)

Suicide and the Soul

A classic introduction to the *experience* of depth psychology—for analyst, patient, and anyone having to meet questions of suicide. Although ostensibly a practical treatise on suicide, it opens into the profound differences between the medical model of therapy and one that engages soul. Since the book's first publication in 1964, it has enjoyed wide recognition in many languages as a teaching text. (191 pp.)

Insearch: Psychology and Religion

Widely used in pastoral counseling and psychotherapeutic training, this book sets out the fundamental attitudes of Jungian psychology in a simple, yet deeply experiential style. Sensitively addresses such topics as listening, curiosity, confession, secrecy, befriending the dream, morality of analysis, conscience, emotions and moods, problems of sexual love, and psychosomatics. (126 pp.)

Loose Ends: Primary Papers in Archetypal Psychology

Twelve papers and talks include "Abandoning the Child," "Nostalgia of the Puer Eternus," "Precursors of Archetypal Psychology," "Betrayal," "Schism," "Masturbation Inhibition," and "Failure and Analysis." Affirms the reality of the psyche and affords an example of subtle, nuanced psychological thought. With notes and/or bibliography appended to each essay. (209 pp.)

The Thought of the Heart

This is an essay on Beauty and the relation between the heart and the world. Part One clears away imprisoning notions of the heart: as muscle and pump, as symbol of royal pride and solar will, as seat of personal sentiments. Part Two relates the heart with the aesthetic response and reactions of outrage at ugliness and injustice. Hillman traces the movements of the heart's failures and its duplicity and then presents a psychology of 'heart operations' that release it from subjectivism and sulphuric illusions so that it can respond like an animal to the ensouled beauty of the sensuous world. (50 pp.)

Spring Publications, Inc. • *P.O. Box 222069* • *Dallas, Texas 75222*